TICKET TO SYRIA

A Story about the ISIS in Maldives

A TICKET TO SYRIA

A Story about the ISIS in Maldives

SHIRISH THORAT

BLOOMSBURY
NEW DELHI • LONDON • OXFORD • NEW YORK • SYDNEY

First published, 2018
This export edition published 2018

BLOOMSBURY PUBLISHING INDIA PVT. LTD.
New Delhi London Oxford New York Sydney

ISBN: 978-93-86826-65-7

10 9 8 7 6 5 4 3 2 1

Published by Bloomsbury Publishing India Pvt. Ltd.
DDA Complex LSC, Building No. 4, 2nd Floor
Pocket 6 & 7, Sector C
Vasant Kunj, New Delhi 110070

Cover photo courtesy of the University of Texas Libraries, The University of Texas at Austin.

Photo by Janko Ferlic on Unsplash.com

Printed and bound in India

This one is for Girish and Arti,
My younger brother and sister in law
Thanks for always having my back

Contents

Author's Note

I first heard of the Maldives when I was allotted a flat at the Police Academy in a village called Jarodakalan on the Delhi-Haryana border. I was told that I was to share a bedroom with a trainee police officer from the Andaman and Nicobar Islands, and across a small bare patch of concrete that passed for a living room was the other bedroom that was allotted to two Maldivians. There was one bathroom with no overhead shower, a single squat toilet and a narrow excuse of a kitchen which was ironic because cooking was not permitted. The four of us exchanged names, shook hands, sized each other up and decided the pecking order for the duration of the training (I was the biggest) and thus started a friendship that would not endure.

We promised to remain in regular touch at the conclusion of the year-long training and that proved impossible. There was a hiatus in communications for many years, *life has an irritable habit of moving on* and I didn't visit the Maldives for the next two decades. We kept in touch more frequently as phone calls grew cheaper and internet services improved and then one day I was in a Sri Lankan airlines aircraft looking out of the window in amazement at the jaw-dropping beauty of every yard that the plane glided over as it approached the landing strip.

The Maldives is vision reinvented; high-end travel brochures regularly have a go at and fail miserably to describe the beauty of its Islands, coral reefs and waters. The fish trace an endless and exquisite pattern of shapes and symmetry and the corals are a living underwater symphony of colours. It is a country blessed by nature with an ecosystem that is as beautiful as it is fragile.

And yet in this paradise society mutates. Despite its very modest population of approximately 350,000, the Maldives has the highest recruitment percentage when it comes to its citizens leaving to engage in a jihad either alongside the Islamic State or the Al-Qaeda. The causal factors are many; unemployment, drug abuse, gang wars and the advent of Salafist ideology being the main contributors. Radicalization is rampant and now plays a role in Maldivian politics.

They say terror has no religion and that may be true, but the biggest weakness of the written and spoken word is that it is prone to misinterpretation and this is paraphrased aptly when Blasé Pascal famously said, *Men never do evil so completely and cheerfully as when they do it from religious conviction*. A cursory glance at medieval and modern history authenticates this observation. Today we stare bemusedly at multiple towers of Babel where ideologies, political correctness, expedient commerce and the narratives of religion and social media produce a cacophony of misinformation.

This book was birthed of a true incident; the names, places and sequence of events have been changed for obvious reasons and I leave it to the reader to determine which parts are fact and what is necessarily fiction. The intent is not just to tell a story but to educate and maybe, just maybe make a difference.

October 2017 **Shirish Thorat**

Acknowledgements

One of life's sobering realities is that there are always people to thank; whatever the task you couldn't do it alone even if you think you have. This is in no particular order or sequence, everyone mentioned here has been invaluable.

Thank you Ridhima Taneja for graciously accepting a late night plea for assistance and to Anu Mehta for recommending her, maybe we will meet some day?

Anil Rodrigues, Bithika Shukla, Mark and Ellen Ross – you guys were my test subjects, I inflicted page after page of typos and grammatically unpalatable manuscripts on you and you were unflinching, I always value your critical feedback.

A big shout out to my friend Manish Kharbikar (IPS Karnataka cadre) for helping me wade through hundreds of pages of mind-numbing research reports and statistical data and highlighting the crucial bits.

My heartfelt thanks to my friends in the Maldives who will have to remain nameless for the present, anything else other than anonymity is sure to earn them a quick trip to the State detention centre at Dhoonidhoo.

Prologue

This was a large group...

Abid Hassan thought as he waited inside his Toyota. His opaque eyes scanned the ragtag bunch and the small nest of vehicles: his Toyota, a minivan and a beat-up Land Rover. He looked to his right across the road and saw nothing of particular interest, just the usual motley collection of human flotsam that congregated around disputed border checkpoints the world over these days. He turned left and saw nothing but endless sand dunes seemingly shrinking and enlarging in turn as the heat waves that roiled upwards distorted his vision.

Yes, perhaps his largest yet...

The group had landed in the Gaziantep sector in Turkey and had assembled at the mausoleum of Sheik Mansour where Abid Hassan had picked them up.

Abid Hassan was more than just a guide; he was the ISIS security Screener for this sector of Turkey. Of late there had been reports of the Khuffar infiltrating the ranks masquerading as recruits for the final Jihad, so Abid doubled as the final security check of all potential soldiers of Allah. There was the big batch from Maldives, he had checked them out, and the recruiter had done a fine job there. The women were young and no doubt fertile and the men fit, and one of them was supposed be of particular value, so much so that he was to be segregated from the rest after the mandatory isolation period everyone had to undergo on crossing into Islamic State territory.

The Islamic State's security Screener for Gaziantep, Abid, was a man of medium height and a prominent belly, the round face and bulbous nose effectively diverting one's attention from the shrewd and intelligent eyes that saw and observed everything, even the minutest changes in posture or expression—but gave away nothing. He had been a document-checker at the Abu Dhabi International airport and knew his way around passports and travel documents. His primary duty was to examine every nuance of a recruit's documentation, background and behaviour. For this he needed to work with the recruiters. It was a relationship which worked on confidence and mutual respect.

As the vehicle grew hotter, the Screener moved his torso closer to the window and felt a welcome draft of semi-cold air from the air conditioner, as it fought a losing battle against the 45-degree Celsius temperature outside it.

The heat was stupefying; it cocooned everything like a seemingly solid blanket of thick air which emanated in waves simultaneously from both earth and sky. It was impossible to look up at the sun; even a glance would blind a man for minutes with yellow and orange fireflies dancing across the retina before the pupils recovered from the shock and started functioning again. To some in the group who weren't used to such climes it was a mental as well as a physical assault on the senses. They would soon grow accustomed, Abid Hassan thought, mentally shrugging his shoulders, as he squinted at a man 50 yards away who had got out of his car and walked into a roadside stall. A minute later, the man came out with a bag of kebabs and bread and got into his car. The outline of the vehicle grew wavy in the heat as it sped away. Abid Hassan looked at his watch again, it was 2.30 pm.

The drive to the border had been uneventful and now they stood waiting just short of the checkpoint at Kilis. They were waiting for the Escort who would take the group into Syria. Abid hunkered over to check the floorboards of the Toyota's front seats yet again. The leather satchel containing the group's passports was still there. This lot was slotted for Raqqa and there was no scope for error.

Abid scanned the Maldives batch once more. There was an infant and a toddler amongst them, apparently an entire family. Abid Hassan's eyes rested on them again. Allah blesses them, he reflected, but he wondered which amongst them would spill their blood on the shores of Dabiq in the final battle and survive, and who would fall along the wayside. There had been so many of the last lately. But then there was obviously no dearth of the devout, a steady stream of humanity came from dozens of countries—men, women, children—all determined to establish the Caliphate or die trying. Everyone had the potential to strike at the Khuffar, indeed the ability to strike in any manner whatsoever itself precluded the possibility of being a non-participant in the Holy War.

A sudden weariness overcame Abid and he slumped in his seat, his head resting briefly against the back of his seat, willing the tension to ooze out as he closed his eyes. Just for a bit, he told himself guiltily, just for a few moments. As usual, in times such as these, his mind flew towards his family or rather his memories of them: *Amma and Abba had died long ago and as for his wife, his lovely Anisa, and their two-year-old...* Abid suddenly tasted bile as his memories soured and he jerked upright to attention. Ah, that was Allah's will, he thought, and resolutely shut a door in his mind to stem the flood, and hunched forward and peered through the windshield scanning the environment again.

This group had made its way into Turkey via Qatar and the watchers there had made their reports to the Screener. None of the group had engaged in suspicious behaviour, he was told. The group had more or less been confined to its rooms in the designated lodgings, and apart from the occasional excursion for purchasing of personal items or foodstuffs, everyone seemed to have behaved. They had adhered to instructions: no cell phones or computers until they reached Raqqa. And no ATM withdrawals either. The electronic signatures and cyber footprints normally generated by travel had to be kept to a minimum to avoid detection.

The cell phone in Abid Hassan's hand buzzed and he glanced at the screen, it was the Escort. 'Salaam,' he greeted the caller.

'Walaikum as-salaam,' the Escort's voice crackled over the phone, 'I should be there in a few minutes, anything for me?'

Abid Hassan paused a second; this was code-speak for 'Are you secure at your end? Anything I should worry about?'

Another searching look around and he spoke into the phone, 'Everything's in great shape here by the grace of Allah.' The phone went silent as the Escort disconnected.

Moisin Shameem was the Escort; he was a tall rangy man of thirty-five, with iron-grey at his temples and the loose loping stride of the desert tribal. He would take the recruits across the last leg of their journey to Al Sham. He lowered the binoculars and blinked in the sudden glare of reflected sunlight, his eyes gradually reverting to their normal focal length. He had been watching the group from the first floor of a building 500 yards away for the last 15 minutes. It was good security to observe the pickup point before initiating contact. That was what he had been taught, and that's the way it would be. Check once, crosscheck and then check once again; it minimized the risk quotient. Moisin Shameem smiled—the number of times he had watched the fat Abid Hassan through these binoculars, that nose and the belly—still smiling, he shook his head. But the man was good; he had to give him that, all these months and not a bad apple, not one. Still, one couldn't become complacent.

Moisin Shameem stepped out of the building and paused. There were no vehicles idling and no passerby seemed out of place. His senses were totally attuned to the environment and his gut told him it was all right. He walked towards the low squat shape of the transport and immigration office with its inevitable pile of sandbags and a sentry on duty. There was no door and he walked in. The Escort was known there and he spent the next five minutes accepting a small cup of the strong local coffee and chatting with the sergeant and the clerk until Abid Hassan walked in. A nod from the Escort and the sergeant took the bunch of passports from Abu and walked to the clerk's desk. The clerk barely glanced at the documents and started stamping them. Moisin casually walked to the sergeant's desk and placed an envelope on it. The envelope was khaki and about half an inch thick. He moved away and a few minutes later, the clerk was done.

***

Abid Hassan collects the paperwork and steps outside. Moisin Shameem joins him and the two men clasp hands and rub noses in greeting. Both are smiling at each other. Inside, the sergeant sweeps the envelope off the table and into a drawer. He looks up and meets the clerk's eyes; both men look at each other without expression.

Outside, Abid Hassan reaches into the folds of his Kandura and hands over a large bundle of SIM cards to Moisin. He delves deep again and comes up with a smaller packet which is sewn tight. It's about 3 inches by 3 and about 2 inches thick. From the precise and minute stitching it's evident that it's a factory job. Abid doesn't know what's inside but he is familiar with such packages. Once, a while ago, he had asked about the contents while making a pickup at the butcher's in Gaziantep, and his query was met with a chilling unblinking stare by the owner. Abid Hassan's abdomen actually contracts at the memory of that stare and he has never asked that question since. He is a man of considerable courage but in this case, by Allah, he doesn't want to know, and he never, ever, in this lifetime wants to be at the receiving end of such a stare again. Despite the heat the memory makes the Screener experience a chill at his temples and the back of his head.

Moisin puts away both items and produces a bunch of what are obviously much-handled envelopes. He gives it to Abid who wordlessly takes them. These would be delivered as per the addresses written on each.

The Moisin makes a quick call and within minutes, three men gather around him. These are the drivers for the final leg of the journey. They would return with the vehicles the next evening to the checkpoint where

Abid Hassan and his men would collect them. As the drivers hurry forward to take charge of the vehicles, the unmistakeable sound of an infant's wail wafts towards them. The Moisin looks at Abid with quizzical eyebrows, Abid shrugs. 'There are two, the other one is a yearling.'

'In this bloody heat?' Moisin's reply is half question-half comment, but he refrains from further speech. He has learnt that a soldier can come in all forms and of all ages. He himself is father to three children. As they near the vehicles the sound of the infant recedes and they can see the mother, a young woman no more than twenty, talking to her baby in the language used by mothers since the time of the first birth.

Moisin looks at the group, and without taking his eyes off it, asks Abid, 'Which one is he?'

'The one in the jeans and cap' Abid replies. 'There... next to the two women, they are his sisters.'

The young man they see is about twenty-three years old, about 5 feet 10 inches, and of slim build. There is a boyish charm to the half-smile on his face. A good-looking young man, his warm brown eyes light up every time he answers his sisters. They in turn obviously adore him. Moisin has seen young men like these before every once in a while. They had a strange glow around them as if they lived charmed lives. So... he thinks, this is the special one and reportedly trained in the US too. He stares at the young man till he looks up and meets his eye. He inclines his head and the boy walks up to him. The Escort places his hands on the boy's shoulders, bends his head and speaks for a long moment into his ear. The two separate, and Moisin comes back to Abid Hassan.

'His name is Aabir,' Moisin says.

'Yes,' his family calls him Abbu,' Abid replies.

'It's time' Moisin says and walks to the minivan. The men don't waste time on goodbyes; there have been so many of those and times were so uncertain these days. Moisin, the Escort, sits next to the driver and the others mount their vehicles too. The small convoy eases onto the road and approaches the checkpoint. Abid Hassan, the Screener for the Islamic State, watches as the sergeant goes through the motions of scrutiny. A few minutes on, the vehicles are already receding towards the horizon. As the last vehicle breasts the gradient, Abid thinks he can hear the infant wailing again.

CHAPTER ONE

Kaalinidhoo, Nonoo Atoll

Sameer Ibraheem is sitting on the sand, about 25 metres away from the changing surf line, his lean bronzed body glistening, the sunlight reflecting off the droplets of water on his arms and shoulders—he has just come out of the sea. He sits with his forearms hugging his knees and gazes outwards towards the ocean, his look unfocused, his entire being absorbing the tiniest susurrations of the energies around him. Like all islanders of Malé, he exults in the feeling of being one with the elements.

A flying fish erupts out of the indigo a hundred yards ahead, its fins flickering, inking a silver tattoo against the horizon for several long moments before diving back into the water with scarcely a ripple. It jolts Sameer out of his reverie and he scans the beach. Muiz, his two-year-old, chases a sandpiper, his face crinkling with the delight which never fails to give Sameer the giddy joy of love as he watches his firstborn run on skinny brown legs, the feet kicking up small fountains of pale sand at every step. Insha'Allah, Sameer prayed, he will grow to be as strong as his father and as beautiful as his mother.

Kaalinidhoo is one of the smaller islands of the Gaanu Atoll with a community of 1,300 souls, a single crescent of tarred road barely a mile in length and two shops that could give you most of what you wanted. A doctor came once every fortnight along with the diesel for the generators and the occasional tourist. The internet was sketchy, alternately boosted and dampened by the winds that swept Kaalinidhoo with an eccentricity that had long since ceased to surprise anyone.

Sameer is the eldest of six siblings, thirty-five years old and the first in the family to go abroad to study and become a doctor. The whole atoll had celebrated the day he had graduated, his father's chest had swollen with pride and his mother kept touching him, ruffling his hair and wiping away her own tears of joy. He has just finished his internship in the hospital in Chennai, India, and is waiting for the health department to give him his marching orders. A newbie was either sent to Bangladesh or Indonesia for a couple of years for experience before they were allotted a government post. The Ibraheems were a wealthy family in the Maldives, but Sameer had always been the oddball of the lot—the one standing in line for the island ferry reading a book and constantly inviting a prod from the person standing behind him to move forward, often to the consternation of others.

He has two brothers and three sisters: Zahara, Zoona and Lena are graduates of the university, and Aabir (Abbu) and Munsiu have ambitions that stretch further. Abbu has just returned from the USA after a year, he is a pilot now. Abbu, with his ear stud and infectious smile, and seemingly endless number of 'foreigner' friends... yes, Abbu has always been his favourite. Munsiu is two years younger than Sameer, and has just married Zahi, his nineteen-year-old bride. Sameer smiles unconsciously, if ever a couple were in love...

'Baba, Baba!' Sameer sees Muiz running towards him holding something in his hand, no doubt he has made another exciting discovery. Every day the child finds a new wonder on the beach. Sameer waits to see today's 'find', maybe an especially colourful seashell or an oddly-shaped cuttlefish bone. The child is like a sponge for information and Sameer prepares himself for the inevitable barrage of questions that will accompany his son's arrival. Just then, his attention is drawn towards the small jetty where he spots the slim figure of his wife waving out to him, obviously beckoning him to come home. As he watches she mimes holding a phone to her ear. Even from this distance he can sense a tension in her carriage and his brow furrows. Sameer gets up at the same time that Muiz reaches him and the child stops short at the expression on his father's face. Sameer takes his hand and father and son walk towards their house in silence, Muiz still clutching the orange-and-black spotted shell that he has found. Behind them the sky grows darker with a red glow outlining the horizon. Islanders believe it portends a storm.

***

Three hours later, Sameer Ibraheem was on the ferry to Malé, the capital of the Maldives, his mind a maelstrom of disbelief and dismay. As the ferry gathered speed and bulled its way through the choppy waters his thoughts struggled to process what he had just heard. The doctor in him was trained to be clinical, to assimilate relevant information and then to analyze it dispassionately, but when he had reached his house earlier, he had been instantly alarmed at the distraught expression on his wife's face. She had been barely coherent and was attempting to string a lucid sentence together when the house phone rang. Sameer walked across the living room to the small alcove that housed the instrument, and a few seconds later, he experienced an onrush of madness entering his world.

The caller had been Ibrahim, his close friend and their neighbour at the family house in Velinidhoo. Ibrahim's voice was uncharacteristically terse.

'Sameer?'

In a few sentences he told Sameer that all his siblings... *all of them*... had left the country to participate in the Jihad in Syria. Munsiu had taken his new bride, and Zoona and Lena had taken their children, the two-year-old Haifa and the three-month-old infant Areef. They had left their husbands behind! Only Zahara had been accompanied by her husband Qassim, a mechanical engineer who ran his own boat-repair yard in the city. According to Ibrahim the entire group had locked the house two days earlier and it was only now that the island grapevine had started buzzing. Sameer mind let out a silent scream of disbelief, and as his wife started wailing, he knew his life would never be the same again.

Sameer's mind flashed back to his parents. They lived in Malé, and his first thoughts were 'How do I tell them?' And 'What do I say?' As he struggled to harness his thoughts another voice had reached him over the phone. It was that of his childhood friend and schoolmate Salim, Salim who was in the police.

'Maa,' Salim said, automatically reverting to the old nickname.

'Salim,' Sameer replied. He was unable to think of anything to say and for a long moment the static crackled over a silent line. Then the voice of the policeman broke the silence.

'Maa, I have confirmed it, they have left, all of them, yesterday morning for Bengaluru. They had an onward flight to Qatar with a connection to Istanbul,' Salim paused, and then continued, 'I have a buddy in the bank who told me Munsiu and Zoona used their cards to purchase the tickets. They are headed for Syria or maybe Iraq.' Another pause and then Salim continued, his voice pitched lower this time, acquiring a conspiratorial tone.

'Maa... I can't do much officially you know and you shouldn't make too many waves either, things are... different these days, as you know.'

'No! I don't know!' Sameer wanted to scream, 'I have just returned from India and before that I was in China, studying....' The rest of the conversation was a blur in his memory. Sameer's cell phone buzzed and he grimaced at the single-bar signal strength notification; cell phone reception was skittish at its best in the islands except when you were in Malé or one of the bigger islands. He walked to the fore where the din of the twin 250 horsepower Yamaha outboards was marginally less, and answered the call. The number displayed on the screen was known to him, it was the one person that he could think of in his circle that could 'get things done.' Sameer wondered why he hadn't thought of Ahmed Idris before.

'Sameer is that you? I have been trying—'

Ahmed Idris is the elder brother of Munsiu's bride and a prominent businessman of Malé. He was also politically connected and a labour leader. In fact, Ahmed had held a ministerial position during the last government and was a friend of Nasheed, the ex-President of Maldives. Things had been 'more modern' during Nasheed's brief tenure.

'Yes, Idris, I am on the ferry, on my way to Malé.' Sameer had to cup his hands around the microphone so that he would be coherent at the other end. Behind him the Yamaha outboards roared unabated and as they cut through the deep blue swell he had to flex his thigh muscles to maintain his balance.

'Good,' Idris's voice came across faintly but steadily, somehow asserting confidence. 'Good,' Idris said again, 'let's meet at my office, give me a call from the jetty once you dock'. There was the crackling of static and Idris' voice came on again: 'Is there anyone else with you?'

'No, I'm alone, why?'

'It would be better if we have a private chat first,

Maa, you understand? With this government we all need to tread softly and carefully.' Idris paused a moment and continued, 'I know you been out of the country and may not realize it, but things have changed, you will find out quickly.'

Another pause and then, 'Anyway, I am waiting for you, we will discuss what to do after you come.'

***

Sameer pockets his phone, turns and stares out at the waters of the Indian Ocean, the blue ovals of his Raybans mirroring a reflection of the ever expanding and receding twin wake-lines of the craft as it slices through the water. He struggles to harness his thoughts; yes, he has been away for some years and returned two months ago. Since his arrival he has spent but a week in the capital and then relaxed at Kalinidhoo. Yes, he has watched TV and surfed the net and yes, he is aware that some misguided souls have left the Maldives for Syria to kill, destroy, burn, rape in order to hack out in his name a bloodsoaked ribbon of land on an earth that was already Allah's. But those must have been fools or fanatics. We don't do these things! his mind screams again, we are educated and peaceful people, we are not... like that. Sameer is suddenly aware that he is weeping, so he turns around again to lean into the wind, gazing with unseeing eyes as he wills Malé closer. After a while he walks to one of the seats and sits staring at the back of the captain's chair. Two hours later they dock at Malé.

The office is a brisk five minutes from the ferry in a building that overlooks the small bathing beach that was specially built a while ago and Ahmed Idris gets up and walks around his desk to meet him. Ahmed wears his trademark white collared T-shirt with jeans. A youthful man of forty, he has applied the benefits of a Western education and a degree in business management from Berkeley to the family trade of ceramics and tuna exports, which has now expanded to resort management. His success is evident in his easy confidence and the opulence of his office. They look at each other for a moment and then embrace. The businessman is the more composed of the two. They sit on the leather sofa and Ahmed Idris begins to talk.

'Have you been in touch with Jaleel and Arshad?' he asks referring to Sameer's other brothers-in-law.

Sameer shakes his head. 'I did call—many times—since I heard... they never answered my calls. I have left messages, too, but... ' his voice trails off.

Idris nods in understanding: the two deserted husbands must be in the throes of extreme humiliation, and to have your wife decamp with your child under such circumstances.... the social stigma must only be exacerbated by the assault on their egos. In Islamic society this was the perhaps the worst ignominy a male could suffer. Idris wondered for an instant how he would have reacted under the circumstances. I don't blame them, he thinks, only last month he had had coffee with both of them. He decides to give them a few days to absorb the shock and maybe then they could meet and discuss the how and why of this......, Sameer head feels like it is going to explode and he has to make an effort to compose himself. Ahmed Idris watches him from across the sofa.

'We can try talking to them again later,' he says. 'The reality is that we can't expect any help from the authorities and we have no clue where or with whom they are presently staying.' Idris leans forward and his eyes lock with Sameer's. 'I made a few calls to my friends in the government and police, and the official attitude is that this is a case of a family voluntarily leaving the country as mere tourists and there is no reason to suspect anything untoward.'

'And what can we expect from your friends unofficially?' Sameer queries, He feels so uneasy talking like this, it's unreal....

Idris replies, his eyes still on Sameer, 'Unofficially, some limited help is possible, very limited. I got the impression that I was already stretching the limits,' His eyes finally drop. 'Nobody wants to know and nobody wants to get involved. I was also obliquely advised not to approach any group or activist—if you get my drift.'

Sameer shakes his head and stands up, he needs to move, he can't sit still. He walks to the window and looks down at the traffic. Without turning his head, he finally speaks, 'So we are basically alone in this? All my siblings are gone, just like that, and we can't do anything?' His voice trails away and he turns to look back at Idris. 'My parents don't know, I will have to tell them somehow.' The prospect looms before him again and he wonders how he is going to do that.

They continue discussing options and make a tentative list of friends on whom they can—maybe—depend, with Idris taking the occasional phone call as business demands. Sameer leaves after an hour and Idris watches from the window as the doctor's slim form weaves its way through the evening crowd on the sidewalk. Idris doesn't envy him his task ahead. The thought of spending any more time in his office suddenly seems unbearable and he leaves for home.

That night Idris senses discomfort around the dining table. Normally, it is an animated spot in the Idris household, the events of the day described to each other, his wife always having some delicious morsel of gossip to share that would leave Ahmed shaking his head in amusement and wonder. It was his wife that had first alerted him to the news in the morning and he had reacted with disbelief.

'What?' he had asked incredulously.

'I heard it from my sister, they have friends at Kaadu.' It was the Island where Zahi lived with her in-laws. 'The house has been locked since the day before and someone saw them at the airport.' She had continued, 'What do I tell my folks? Oh, this is so shameful!'

That of course had evoked an angry response from Idris and the resultant tears and recriminations had only exacerbated things and set the tone for the rest of the day.

His wife is now asking no more questions and the conversation starts and stops in spurts, grabbing at inane and valueless ideas that fizzle out within moments of initiation. She goes to bed early and Idris sits staring sightlessly at the TV, his eyes unfocused and his mind on his little sister Zahi, who had been educated in Singapore and who loved her collection of Katy Perry and Adele and who preferred wearing jeans to the hijab, how could she do something like this?

Did she not know what lay ahead for her and her husband? Where was she right now, was she even alive? Idris's heart feels as if someone has squeezed it. He gets up, switches off the television, walks into his study and locks the door behind him. From a drawer at his desk he removes a bottle of Grey Goose vodka and pours himself a stiff drink. He adds ice from the small refrigerator that hums in the corner and returns to his desk. Alcohol is illegal in the Maldives except in the resorts, but those who drank usually had a stash. Well, Idris thinks, as he takes a sip and lets the chilled liquid roll around his tongue, Allah will forgive me this one. He prepares himself for the phone call he knows he has to make.

***

There are people in our lives that we hope not to have to turn to for help—and sometimes have to. These persons are like the mongoose one has in the backyard to take care of the snakes. One can't keep a mongoose as a pet but one needs it just in case. In societal parlance such persons are called 'contacts'—but this contact is my friend, thinks Idris as he starts scrolling on his cell phone for the name. I have never asked him for anything... until now. And yet how little I know of him except that he has that weird almost elemental aura about him and then also, there was the way he had handled that business back in 2007. The instant he had heard the news about Zahi, Idris had known that only that man amongst his many friends could help him.

Idris finds the name; the last time they met they had snorkelled carrying spear guns, later they had barbecued their catch. Idris smiles at the memory. He has never enjoyed a day so much since. He doesn't hesitate now because he sees no one else that he has any confidence in. And so, Idris shifts the Grey Goose a few inches nearer and touches the green icon. Some 9,000 miles away a phone starts to ring.

CHAPTER TWO

The small brown pellets hit the surface with barely audible plops and almost immediately there is a swirl of movement in the water. As usual it's the white one with the black spots which rises first, followed by the others, it has always been bolder than the rest and now its head breaks the surface and the mouth opens, it gathers three of the pellets and he watches the flick of the tail as it dives downwards again. The red and white ones are easy to spot and the purely white ones appear to be greyish or silver depending upon the light. There is one that is red and white with black stripes that reminds him of a tiger; it has the same compact symmetry of shape and size. Within a minute there are no more pellets floating and the koi circle the pond expectantly. The second flurry of pellets follows, delivered by a practised flick of the wrist.

It's not a big pond, just 7 feet wide and about 9 feet long, and the Contact has built the filtration system himself. It hasn't been a resounding success and every few days the water tends to cloud up with algae which means he has to clean the lava rocks he chose as a filter medium. It's wet and dirty work and results more often than not in the occasional scraped elbow or hand, but he doesn't mind. The koi comfort him and he hopes that one day they will nibble the pellets right out of his hand. Many years ago he watched monks feeding the fish at a Japanese shrine. Do that once and the memory stays with you.

The Contact walks across to check the blue plastic box he has used to house the filter to inspect it for leaks. He is a tall man, easily in excess of six feet in height, and lean of build. He wears a loose shirt that has seen better days and a leather belt tightened to the last notch, the jeans are obviously a very loose fit. This, combined with the spread of his shoulders and the width of his bony joints hint at a man who was perhaps much bigger once. He lives in a modest A-framed house in a lane; similar, modest, A-frame houses dot the East coast. It is of early 19th-century vintage and largely constructed of wood. There are parks and shops within a few minutes' driving distance and New York City is just an hour away. It's a quiet neighbourhood and strangers stand out immediately, rabbits abound and the occasional deer peek over the fence. The backyard hosts a solitary leafy elm, its shade welcome in the summers.

The Contact has built a rough seat of brick and concrete at the edge of the pond and sits on it now with a handful of dried shrimp that he purchases at the nearby Chinese supermarket. It's a once-a-day special treat, and the Contact grins in anticipation as he flicks some in. The koi as usual go crazy and engage in aquatic battle for the almost weightless flattened flakes of pure protein. He leans forward in anticipation when the dog comes out on to the deck and barks at him. It's a large dog, and an obvious variant of the German shepherd breed.

'What is it?' he asks and the dog barks again, this time looking back into the house. 'Must be someone at the front door,' the Contact mutters to himself. He climbs the wooden steps leading up to the deck which overlooks the backyard and enters the house. The dog runs ahead and comes to a halt at the study table with its untidy and motley collection of books and papers. On top of a pile of magazines, a mobile phone lies with its screen still glowing blue. The Contact picks it up, there is a missed call notification, it's Idris from the Maldives and his eyes crinkle as he smiles, it has been a while he thinks. Just then the phone starts buzzing. It's Idris again. The Contact speaks into the phone.

'Hello, my friend, how are you?' he asks.

Idris's voice comes across the ether, faint but coherent: 'Unfortunately, things are not okay, my friend.' Idris pauses and the Contact can hear his friend swallow, followed by the definitive sound of a glass being placed on a table. He glances at the digital clock on the cable TV's DVR; it is 10.45 pm in the Maldives and Idris is having a drink on a weekday. The Contact's brow furrows.

'I need your advice and help,' Idris continues. 'I never ever thought this sort of thing would happen to my family,' Idris's voice breaks 'I... '

The Contact interrupts, 'Hold it, Ahmed, tell me what happened.' He speaks in a clipped and measured tone. 'Now start again, from the beginning, as it happened.'

Five minutes on, Idris has said all there is to say. It's a trait of logic that an entire array of seemingly overwhelming and insurmountable issues can be reduced to a few sentences. The Contact's unhurried voice has kick-started Idris's left brain and he has automatically risen to match its linear thinking. Idris waits calmly for his friend to speak.

The Contact settles back in his own chair and speaks tersely. 'You have a pen and paper handy? Good, now listen.'

As he speaks, Ahmed Idris begins to scribble furiously on the notepad on his lap.

'The first thing you do is get another number under a friend's or employee's name, till such time we can talk on Viber or Whatsapp. Open up a Gmail chat account and we can use that too, on occasion. Now I don't want you to meet with Sameer in person anymore. It's for *his* safety, I am sure he is under some sort of loose surveillance and I don't want you appearing on anyone's radar, you understand?'

At at the other end, Idris nods, and after a second replies, 'Yes, I understand.'

'Ask Sameer to go to the family house, where they once all lived, and conduct a search, tell him to search the perimeter around the house and the trash bins also, I want a list of all items that the vanished members have taken with them, particularly all electronic items. Tell him to look for covers, boxes and wrappings indicating new purchases; there could be brochures and instruction manuals, receipts lying around or in the garbage. Also I want their mobile numbers, email addresses, social media details like Facebook, Twitter, Instagram etc. Got that?

'Yeah, I am noting it all down,' says Idris. 'Just go a bit more slowly.'

'I want Sameer to get their bank and credit card details, there must be old bills and statements lying around in the house, ask his policeman friend to go to the bank if need be, we must know how much cash they are carrying or if they made any large withdrawals or transfers recently.

'Send me their photographs, passport details, educational details, particularly the pilot's, get me the number he used when he was in America.' Another pause, 'Ask Sameer to report the matter to the police station for whatever it is worth. He is to also write a letter to the Ministry of Foreign Affairs, just giving names and his suspicions—nothing more—it doesn't matter if they take cognizance or not, but I want it on record.'

As Ahmed Idris writes down the instructions he feels an enveloping sense of calm. Yes, he thinks, I did the right thing. And for the first time in 24 hours he feels hope.

The Contact's voice breaks into his reverie again. 'I will text you another number, give it to Sameer and ask him to contact me on Whatsapp and Viber, I will use that number only with him. I also want the call details of the entire groups' cell phones for the last three months, if possible…if not, then certainly for the last seven or eight weeks, that's vital.

'And… yes, another thing, ask Sameer to locate the travel agent who booked the tickets and instruct him to make enquiries as to who came to collect the tickets, how did they pay for it… there may be CCTV on the premises. Try and get the footage, it's a long shot but maybe someone bought the tickets for them or accompanied them there.

'I also want to know,' the Contact goes on, 'if there was a layover in Bengaluru or Qatar. Travel itinerary would show that, therefore the ticketing details are important.'

'Understood,' Idris replies, his eyes running over the list the Contact has just reeled off. It reads like a shopping list, Idris thinks wryly. Shaking his head in amazement, he hears the Contact speak again, as if guessing Idris's thoughts. 'I know this is quite a bunch of things to do but get it done as quickly as you can and call me on Viber once you have something for me' The Contact's tone changes, more gentle now as he says, 'Don't worry, my friend, I will do all that I can, you know that.'

'Yes... yes, I know that,' Idris's voice thickens with emotion.

'So call me later—and don't empty that bottle of vodka,' the Contact chuckles and clicks off.

***

He sits in the chair for a long time, his mind replaying the conversation of the last half hour. He knows the world he is about to enter intimately, every volatile, fetid and traitorous corner of it; indeed he had chosen to stand at its epicentre and view it with a dispassion that would insulate him from any more grief and hurt. And now… now this. The Contact shrugs; one cannot dodge one's *kismet* and this is mine and, well then, so be it.

That afternoon the Contact takes the metro to the city and then the subway to the lower Manhattan Chinatown. He walks through the fish markets on Mott Street occasionally inspecting the wares, and then enters Canal Street with its row of costume jewellers and shops selling knockoffs of perfumes and electronics. A visit to a small back alley shop and 45 dollars get him a grey-market cell phone and a prepaid SIM card with a hundred minutes talk time on it. Neither item can be traced to him and anyway, he would be dropping them into a storm drain in five days and buying another set. It was cheap and sensible security. He returns home and goes for his evening walk in the park nearby.

Later that evening he switches on his laptop and surfs the internet deep into the night, occasionally he makes a call, Idris and Sameer would be calling tomorrow and there was a lot to be done before they did. As the Contact works, the dog slumbers lightly at his feet, its ears twitching at the small night sounds that come from the backyard.

CHAPTER THREE

The Contact woke up early the next morning. He hated doing that so when the alarm started buzzing he ignored it for a while before reaching over and silencing it, quickly checking for any missed calls since he slept with the phone on mute. After decades of broken slumbers thanks to the insistent ringtones of phones at all odd hours he felt that he owed himself this small luxury. He had made an appointment for an extended brunch with an old acquaintance, someone he always consulted as an expert when it came to politics and terrorism vis-à-vis the Middle Eastern theatre.

Liyaqat Chowdhary (that was the name the Contact knew him by) was a lesser-known goldmine of knowledge when it came to Islamic studies and the ideological differences between the bewildering varieties of radical Islamic terrorism. Liyaqat lived in a small farm in Albany with his Iranian wife who, the Contact remembered from past experience, was a dreadful cook, her piéce de rèsistance being a dish she called chicken polo. The Contact mentally shuddered at the memory of burnt rice with pieces of chicken that took forever to chew. He would stop at the local halal shop and pick up a few pounds of their best biryani as a 'gift'; no doubt the long-suffering Liyaqat would put in a special mention for him in his prayers that evening.

Grinning at the thought, the Contact swung his legs to the floor, it was a long drive to Albany and he wanted to beat the commuter traffic. Half an hour later he was ready. The dog looked at him with questioning eyes. 'No, you are not coming along, Muslims don't like dogs in their houses.' He made sure that the dog's water bowl was topped up, tossed some feed in the koi pond and left the door to the yard open.

A few minutes later he swung into the fast lane of the Garden State parkway—he would reach his destination in four hours.

Liyaqat Chowdhary was a short spare man; he was always neatly dressed and fastidious about his beard which was so immaculate in its proportions, that the Contact was convinced that Liyaqat used a pair of vernier calipers to groom it to the desired shape and size every morning. He received the packed biryani from his friend with a gleaming smile and a conspiratorial wink. His wife came in and greetings were exchanged, after which she ducked out and the Contact didn't see her for the rest of his visit. Liyaqat ushered his guest onto the patio overlooking the stream that meandered behind the house. They sat under the awning on comfortable chairs and upon Liyaqat's insistence, the Contact removed his shoes. He asked for and got a small notebook and a pen. Without further ado, the Scholar on Middle Eastern affairs began to talk. Both men had done this before and knew each other's habits. The Contact would rarely interrupt except to ask for clarity when he failed to grasp a particular nuance or context.

'On Sunday 29 June 2014, the first day of the holy month of Ramadan, Abu Mohammed al-Adnani, the official spokesperson of Islamic State, announced the restoration of the Çaliphate and the renaming of its group to the Islamic State (IS) via a public audio message. The newly established Islamic State had made major appropriations in Iraq, including the capture of key cities, oil refineries, weapons and military armaments, and approximately $450 million in gold and cash looted from banks and treasury vaults in these areas. Within a few weeks the Islamic State would come to control an area roughly the size of the United Kingdom.

'Note,' added Liyaqat, 'that I call it the Islamic State as opposed to ISIS, or as the Americans prefer, ISIL, as while, in my mind, this organization has already taken on the configurations of a State, many others would not want to refer to it as IS to risk legitimizing the phrase or to inadvertently lend credence to the IS rhetoric.'

'After all'—Liyaqat leaned forward, his eyes locked with the Contact's—'how does one define a country in international law? I understand that physical dominance over a specified land mass and a population that is compliant to a set of laws would constitute a country. Would it not?' The Scholar pressed home his point. 'In this respect the Islamic state is not different to Israel or South Sudan, one may argue, or any other country for that matter. It is this fact that the West seeks to obfuscate by labelling this phenomenon as terrorist.'

Liyaqat paused and in a mannerism familiar to the Contact's, he steepled his fingers and tilted his head slightly to the right. He was warming to his narrative.

'The Western world professed to have been taken by surprise but the truth is that they were blind to events occurring daily and did not heed the warning signs, The rise of IS wasn't a freak chain of circumstances but rather a slow and gradual gathering of events and social development that created—for want of a better phrase—'the perfect storm of Islamic terrorism'. I would say there are five main reasons for this.

'Firstly,' Liyaqat raised a forefinger, 'one must consider the fact that the Arab world has been for some time undergoing a rapid change in terms of rising Islamist fundamentalism, declining sense of nationalism and a sense of empowerment spurred by the so-called Arab Spring phenomenon. The Islamic State is a physical manifestation of that draconian belief.'

'Secondly, following the regimes' collapse in Iraq and Syria there were no acceptable substitutes. The resultant power vacuum in the Sunni regions of the two states paved the way for an alternative governing force to coalesce, gain momentum, acquire acquiescence and finally the active support of the civilian population.'

Liyaqat raised another portentous finger. 'Thirdly—and mark the irony—this is a case of the information age meeting the dark age, the use of the internet as a platform for social networking makes it easier for people to communicate across large distances to share experiences, information and also to discuss beliefs with like-minded individuals. It also enables a believer to actively persuade others to sympathize with or join a cause.'

Liyaqat continued, 'Another unexpected contributor is the global phenomenon of climate change. There have been consistently long periods of droughts in both these States. Over the last decade this has wreaked havoc on the region's economic and social stability.' Liyaqat now held his palm outward with all his fingers spread out.

'Finally,' he extended his thumb upward, 'we have what is commonly referred to as the "Youth bulge". Syria and Iraq are experiencing a surge in the percentage of young people that, when combined with severe unemployment and lack of political expression, has resulted in a large reserve of very angry and unemployed youth which is close to bursting point.'

The Contact was listening with rapt attention. He made it a point to keep up with global affairs but this visit was to get a professional and in-depth view into terrorism. His own expertise, however dated, lay in the immediately related field of counterterrorism, but now, with the Maldives affair on his hands... the Contact believed in doing his homework and so he listened with concentration to Chowdhary. It would help him appraise the situation better.

'Now,' Liyaqat went on, 'the Islamic State's capacity to control is based on several factors. It has monopoly over the use of force in the area it governs. It uses implicit and explicit threat of violence against civilians to ensure acquiescence. Punishments for transgressions are swift and brutal. On the other hand, one can reasonably make a case that the Islamic State provides better governance, administration, essential services, and provides a degree of stability and order in a previously very uncertain environment.

'When one considers the reality of a total absence of any viable Sunni-empowered governance, then the Islamic State emerges as a plausible alternative, feeding on the collective need for a Sunni identity and redressal of similarly perceived grievances.

'Am I making myself clear?' Liyaqat asked abruptly.

The Contact nodded in acquiescence and the scholar of Middle Eastern politics continued. 'The Islamic State has demonstrated a strong, flexible and versatile leadership and organizational structure which has a highly motivated and dedicated rank and file of disciplined cadre. This is bolstered by a phenomenally effective social media and recruitment strategy. Its spread of ideology and ability to survive coalition attacks goes a long way in convincing Sunni Muslims and local power brokers of its longevity.

'The Islamic State's narrative is that Muslims around the world have a moral imperative to support them. It uses shared feelings of marginalization, repression, victimization and lack of power at the hands of Shias and the West to gain support. The fact that the Islamic State actually holds sway over real physical land gives it a considerable measure of legality. It brings in a sense of immediacy as opposed to the Al-Qaeda core narrative, that it needed to wait for the right time to establish a caliphate. The Islamic State accomplished this within months and touts it as irrefutable evidence of its willingness to take action with immediate effect.

'The Islamic State offers thrills, adventure and opportunity for heroism and violence, all of which appeal to a cadre of young men's sense of masculinity. It doesn't hold one's past life against someone as long as they embrace and live by their interpretation of Sharia in this one. So, you could say that the Islamic State offers a reinvention of self.'

Liyaqat paused dramatically and then said, 'And so, my friend, this confluence of geopolitical and geosocial causes and effects is primarily responsible for the emergence and success of the Islamic State and in fact...'

The Scholar's monologue was interrupted by the buzz of the Contact's new cell phone. He looked at the screen. It was Idris.

'Excuse me,' he said to Liyaqat, 'I have to take this one.' His host nodded and the Contact walked inside.

'Hello, Ahmed. Anything?'

'Yes,' replied Idris. 'Sameer searched the house as you directed, he found empty jackets of 10 SIM cards, they had been purchased less than a week ago. The interesting thing is that they show up in the names of random non-Muslim monikers. In fact, they seem to be registered in the names of tourists to the Maldives.'

The Contact's eyebrows rose slightly as he considered the information. He knew it indicated organization and planning. To be able to arrange 10 SIM cards under assumed names... he shelved the thought as Idris continued.

'They have taken all their laptops, and Sameer couldn't find the hard drive in the desktop computer. He did get some account details and is going to the bank in Malé tomorrow.' Idris paused for breath. 'It turns out that the tickets were bought in two lots from two different travel agencies. I assume that was to avoid attracting attention.'

'Anything else?' the Contact asked, tersely.

'No, I am having Sameer work on the other points,' replied Idris.

'Okay, two more things from my side,' said the Contact hurriedly. 'Firstly, find out if anyone has a medical condition that may require any specific prescription drug, if so then send me the details,' the Contact instructed Idris. 'Also, send me a few pictures of their house, one taken from the outside and a couple of the inside exactly the way they left it, do you understand?'

At the other end, Idris replied in the affirmative, quick to grasp the reason behind the latest demand from his friend. They ended the call and the Contact walked out to sit under the awning, smiling reassuringly at Liyaqat and pouring himself a glass of water. As the Contact settled back with his notepad once more, Liyaqat resumed his delivery.

'At its core, the Islamic State wants to restore the Caliphate, a centuries-old notion of a world governed by Sharia law and ruled by a caliph, someone considered to be a successor to the Prophet Mohammad's political authority. Abu Bakr al-Baghdadi, the forty-six-year-old Iraqi who broke away from Al-Qaeda in 2013, is such a man. Baghdadi is the self-proclaimed Caliph Ibrahim II, ostensibly tracing his lineage to Caliph Ibrahim I, who ruled the Ottoman Empire from 1640 to 1648. In order to increase his legitimacy on that score, he uses the additional name "al-Qurayshi".'

Liyaqat stopped to pour himself a glass of water and put a slice of the freshly cut lemon, that his wife had placed in a dish, he added a couple of ice cubes to top up the drink, and both men watch the condensation form on the glass. The Scholar took a small swallow and resumed.

'Now, my friend, you have to understand that the caliph is an incredibly important symbolic figure in Islamist terms and the reestablishment of the caliphate has been an objective for all Islamist and jihadist groups, from the Muslim Brotherhood in Egypt to the Jemaah Islamiyah in southeast Asia. The caliphate has total religious and political jurisdiction over the entire Muslim populace, or *ummah*, as it is called in Arabic.'

'Although the Islamic State is a highly centralized and disciplined organization, its size and the extent of territory it controls makes delegation essential. Abu Bakr has operational heads in charge of different theatres like Iraq, Syria, Sinai, Afghanistan and Libya.

A specialized 'war office' manages the logistics and technicalities of war. Baghdadi has shown himself to be willing to delegate responsibility and to rely on the skills of his subordinates. That has demonstrated the advantages of autonomous decision-making, since many of his commanders have served as high-ranking officers in Saddam Hussein's military and have high-level technical expertise. This military expertise is reflected at all levels of the Islamic State's war machine. There are approximately 1,000 medium-to-top-level field commanders right now even as we speak.'

'Baghdadi sets the overall strategic objectives of the group, which are then passed down through the hierarchy with each lower rung in turn having a degree of autonomy in their fulfilment. This is especially true in military operations where a local commander will know what he has to achieve, and even where to attack, but the exact timing and method may be left to his discretion. This system of devolved authority has enabled the Islamic State to operate on many fronts simultaneously, both administratively and militarily. The appointed councils are responsible for the military and administrative organization of the Islamic State, giving counsel to Baghdadi and overseeing strategic planning, military operations, and civilian administration.'

Liyaqat seemed lost in reflection for a long moment. The Contact wondered if he should prod him into speaking when Liyaqat gave himself a little shake and took up the thread of his talk.

'In Islam,' he intoned, 'religion is law. And it is this conundrum that confronts the Western world when it comes to understanding the Islamic State and its followers. The rest of the world practises their respective religions according to their faith whilst adhering to a common code of conduct that we call the law of the land—our set of dos and dont's, if you will. The Islamic State supplants law with the Sharia and this is enforced by the Sharia Council which is the most powerful body, and directly overseen by Abu Bakr al-Baghdadi. It has six members. It is responsible for selecting a caliph and enforcing the compliance of all parts of the administration with Sharia law, according to its own interpretation. It is assisted by the Sharia Commissions ensuring party discipline, formation of rules, code of conduct, deciding penalties for any infringements, supervising the Sharia police and courts and overseeing ideological outreach (known as da'wa), both in areas under the State's control and beyond.'

'Does argument or discourse enter into any of this?' It was a short question the Contact had been harbouring for a long while.

'The Islamic State, being totalitarian by nature, has zero tolerance towards dissent,' answered the Expert without preamble. 'Naturally, therefore, there is a Security and Intelligence Council which is primarily responsible for eliminating al-Baghdadi's rivals. This council plays a vital role in maintaining and asserting his control, as well as ensuring his physical security. The Security Council has a network of branches throughout the State. In the beginning, it controlled about 20 people, but it expanded rapidly after that as it assassinated defectors and otherwise eliminated any challenges to the organization, from local leaders, activists, religious scholars and the like.'

The flutter of wings distracted both men and they shifted in their chairs to watch a black-and-white bird with a red crest settle on the corner post. 'It's a Ladderback woodpecker, the Contact observed. 'It's common here in upstate New York.' Both men admired the bird's barred plumage and the quick jerky movements of its scarlet head. Apparently finding nothing of interest, the bird flew away and the Expert was able to pursue the subject.

'Then there is the Military Council that drives the campaign to win more territory and defend what is already held. In this it is helped by the Provincial Council, which oversees the civilian administration of the State through its 18 provinces which are called *wilayats*. In addition, there are the Finance Council, the Media Council, and a council that looks after fighters and their families.' Liyaqat chuckled darkly. 'So you see, my friend, we have quite the little government going on there.'

'In the administration of its territories, the provincial system allows a measure of independence to local governors who are liable to be moved from place to place with some frequency to prevent the growth of power bases independent of the central leadership. Below the level of governor, who is known as *Wali*, the provinces have an administrative stream and a services stream. The first covers Islamic outreach, Sharia institutes, religious education, a very severely controlled non-religious education, law enforcement, courts, recruitment, and security and tribal affairs. The services stream, known as the Islamic Administration of Public Services, looks after the region's infrastructure, including electricity, sanitation, water, agricultural irrigation systems, cleaning and repairing of roads, humanitarian aid and other essential services such as the production of bread, etc. In this respect, through the seizure of grain stores, it has reportedly been able to lower prices and keep bakeries running. Its monopoly of services provides the State with a further means of control over the population and easy opportunities to penalize dissent.'

The Contact waited, thirsty for more of the details that few like this man could provide. The Scholar settled himself more comfortably in his chair and smiled ironically at his friend. The shadow of the awning gradually shortened and the day grew warmer.

CHAPTER FOUR

They had stopped for an hour at Manbij, at a fuel station, the ladies using the facility of the toilets while Moisin the Escort supervised the loading of some wooden crates onto the Toyota Hilux. Manbij was also known as 'Little London' on account of the number of Muslims from the United Kingdom who had chosen to be Mujahirs and travelled here to defend the territory, it was also an important IS stronghold in the Northern Syrian sector and a vital hub in the logistics and supply chain from Turkey to Raqqa. An hour, and they were underway again. Now, six hours after passing through the checkpoint at Kilis the convoy veered to the right, off the highway that ran parallel to the Euphrates river and headed into Raqqa. Fifteen minutes later, the vehicles halted behind the old Armenian church which now served as an administrative headquarters for the Islamic State. The Escort got out of his Toyota and walked across the street to an adjacent building that served as the recruitment and registration office for the province.

The IS maintains multiple recruitment offices for military service in each province. Any Muslim who wants to enter the fighting corps of the army of the State is welcomed. There is, of course, a well-drawn-out security process in place to identify and deal with any attempts of embedding or infiltration by rival groups or the Khuffar. The recruitment offices handle registration of potential candidates, who are then put through the phases of 'Sharia and military preparation' before being sent to the battlefront. The State also maintains dedicated training camps for children, including one named 'Cubs of Zarqawi' in the Eastern Ghouta region of Damascus. Unlike a typical jihadist group, the Islamic State openly broadcasts the locations of its recruitment centres in Syria. This is because it sees itself not as a terrorist organization, but as an actual state attempting to recruit citizens into its standing army.

The Escort saw the registration officer at his usual place, behind a wooden desk with his laptop. He was a small bespectacled man who always had a mug of coffee next to him. The laptop was connected to a printer and had a 1TB external hard disk attached to it. He looked up as the Escort greeted him.

'Salaam,' he said in reply, and indicated a chair beside him.

'Well, the lot is waiting outside' the Escort spoke, his body visibly relaxing in the chair as he sat down. 'You want to send someone out to get them, or shall I?'

The officer reached over and pressed a switch. Moments later a staff member answered the bell and was instructed to bring the group in. A few minutes later, they entered, the infant silent, presumably asleep. A couple of female staff joined them as each person filled up his or her registration form. The columns required details that one would usually furnish when applying for, say, a passport or a tourist visa. Each member was required to note down details of their name, sex, date of birth, address, family details, educational qualifications, photograph, special skills set, social media and email details, and finally names and contact details of relatives in their country of origin. There were other details to be disclosed—such as the blood group, if the citizen wanted to become a martyr, or warrior, or if the citizen wanted to serve in any other specific way.

There were a few voices that demurred when it came to giving up their cell phones and password details for emails and social media, but the officer said that those were required for a couple days only, primarily for verification and a scrutiny of their social media profile. The forms would be examined for objectionable content or elements that may pose a security risk to the Islamic State. They could, the officer further elaborated, always change the password after a few days. The contact details of one's family, he went on to explain, were required to communicate details of their well being (or not) to their near and dear ones back in the country of their origin. Such details had other uses as well. Nevertheless, it took less than half an hour to fill up the forms and they were placed in a neat pile on the wooden desk. The details would be fed into the wilayat database later.

The officer thumbed through the forms till he found the one he wanted. This one he placed in the drawer in his desk. He would attend to that one

later. His instructions were to change the details and switch the photograph on that one, he didn't know why, he didn't care. He received such instructions every once in a while and he complied with them. This one was to be shifted to another base after the initial period and then... he knew not where. This group, like all the others, would undergo the basic Sharia and military training according to their sex, and skill sets, and then would be deployed as deemed fit. It was, the registration officer thought, all part of the caliph's vision.

Maldives

Sameer Ibraheem sat on a bench in the reporting room of the police station in Malé, the capital; he had been sitting for two hours with his folder of documents waiting for someone to come and talk to him. Earlier, he had spent an hour writing down an appeal to the state machinery about his predicament—it was in part an appeal and also a notice—and from the look of things it wasn't welcome. He had felt it since the time he had approached the sergeant on duty. The sergeant had looked up and Sameer imagined he saw a fleeting expression of recognition in the man's eyes.

'Yes,' the sergeant had asked, 'how may I help you?'

Sameer proffered his written appeal with an outstretched arm, 'I have to file a missing report of my family.'

'Your family?' the sergeant pointedly refused to look at the sheaf of papers Sameer was holding out and continued, 'Your family?... Your wife is missing?'

'No, it's my brothers and sisters. Along with two children—one is just an infant—also my brothers' wives,' Sameer began to explain, but the sergeant cut him short.

'You mean you cannot trace them? Did they have a boating accident?'

'No, they haven't, you see, they left three days ago for India and then they…' again the interruption from the sergeant.

'Oh, so you know where they are? Then what is the problem?'

The conversation went south from there on and a short argument later, Sameer was asked to sit on the bench until 'the senior officer arrives'.

The sergeant had gone to a phone at the other end of the large reporting room and made a call; he had thereafter resumed his duties and steadfastly ignored Sameer. Another fifteen minutes ticked by with excruciating slowness for the islander. So this is how it is going to be, Sameer thought, I can expect more of this, certainly.

'You,' the sergeant's voice broke into his reverie and Sameer looked up. 'The chief inspector wants to see you.'

Sameer followed him through a series of short and long corridors until they came to a room at the rear of the building. A knock at the door, and a command to enter followed. The sergeant stepped in, followed by Sameer and snapped to attention. A quick salute, and the sergeant exited, leaving Sameer standing awkwardly in front of the desk of the chief inspector. He didn't know which the appropriate way was of approaching the inspector's desk. There were a dozen chairs lined up in three rows in front of the inspector's desk so the choice was either from the near or the far end. As Sameer stood hesitating, the inspector waved him vaguely to the right, and Sameer guessed his way to a chair.

Less than half an hour later, tempers were already frayed, evident in the inspectors voice. 'You see, Mr Ibraheem,' he gritted between his teeth, 'I *can't* register a missing report because your family *isn't* missing. They went *out* of the Maldives, you told us that yourself. There is no suspicion of foul play because by all appearances they went voluntarily. As for the married women… well, their husbands haven't come with you so I really can't comment… Now you say they have left to go to Syria to wage jihad? Do you know against whom, may I ask? What evidence is there to that effect? Have they communicated that intent? No, no, Mr Ibraheem, I cannot see any criminal element in this. What I see is that a family has decided to take a vacation, and nothing else.'

Sameer interrupted, 'But surely you can't believe, sir, that a large, well-to-do family would just up and leave like this? You know that many Maldivians have left for jihad to Syria, it has been the trend these last two....'

'Now wait a minute' the inspector interjected forcefully, leaning forward for the first time, 'there is no basis in what you say. First of all, there is *no*—as you claim—trend of Maldivians engaging in jihad, so don't go around spreading dangerous rumours, Mr Ibraheem.'

'These are not rumours, sir,' Sameer said. 'Look at the newspapers. There were so many reports about that in the last year.'

'Oh, those are antinational forces up to their usual mischief. I am the chief of police and *I* am telling you that there is nothing of the sort going on. I suggest you go home, and I am sure they will come back. These things happen sometimes, you know.'

Sameer could see that this wasn't getting anywhere. He thought for a few moments and then said, 'At least accept this report, and verify with the resources at your disposal.' The inspector shook his head in irritation and both men looked at each other doggedly. Clearly, it was an impasse.

Finally, the officer spoke. 'Well, all right, I will ask the sergeant to accept your application, but please note that as far as I am concerned it's for the sake of information only. I do not intend to interfere with the decision of a bunch of adults who have decided to leave for an impromptu vacation. So please don't expect anything else from me.'

The inspector pressed a switch and the sergeant entered the room. The inspector handed the papers to him with the instruction, 'Just acknowledge receipt and file them.' The sergeant nodded and left. Sameer made to follow him when the officer spoke again. 'Mr Ibraheem, I suggest you go home to your wife and child. I understand you have just returned from abroad.' Sameer nodded, his skin crawling as he listened to the inspector's voice telling him, 'Obviously, you have had various kinds of exposure while studying abroad. That's good, travel expands the mind but… this is an Islamic country, you understand? Be a good Muslim, Ibraheem, and everything will be all right. Stay healthy, and *safe*.

Numbly, Sameer stepped out into the corridor. The sergeant took a couple of minutes to peruse the application and rubber-stamped a copy in acknowledgement, handing the copy to Sameer and, staring steadily at him as he did so. Wordlessly, Sameer accepted the papers. As he walked out of the air-conditioned reporting room of the police station, he was aware that his forehead was dripping with perspiration.

Raqqa

In Arabic, *al-Da'wa* literally means 'the call', and it devolves upon Muslims to formally call all others to Islam. The IS conducts religious outreach as one of its first actions upon entering a new

territory. The Da'wa events, complete with camps, Quranic recitations, and religious sermons are formulated to engage participants in the State's core beliefs. Da'wa events are often single sessions and therefore require little investment in resources, thus they are a logical first choice for the IS when it seeks to establish a foothold in a particular area. In addition, because the Da'wa events are non-threatening and often involve providing food and drink to the population, there is scant possibility of causing any serious backlash. A vital component of the State's religious outreach programme is the management of Sharia institutes within its territories. In practice, these institutes function much like adult education centres, providing a space where Muslims can learn about 'the core of their religion'. The State has also established specialized institutes for women only.

Once Da'wa programmes make inroads into a territory and the IS makes an official entry, the role of the religious police (*Al-Hisba*) assumes importance. Unlike local police forces, Al-Hisba has a mandate to 'promote virtue, prevent vice, dry up sources of evil, nip signs of non-adherence in the bud and urge Muslims towards well-being'. Al-Hisba members are also responsible for documenting alleged violations of Sharia in order to 'rectify issues and find suitable solutions'. Serious violations such as insulting, Islam or the Prophet are all referred to the local Islamic court for adjudication.

The officer was aware that the Islamic State had invested considerably in the Al-Hisba infrastructure both in Aleppo and Raqqa provinces. This tool, more than any of the State's other instruments of governance, directly impacted the lives of civilians, established a strict code of conduct and violently punished those who failed to conform. Naturally, the objective of Da'wa was to establish firm territorial control and boost popular support for itself with other governance activities before instituting a robust Al-Hisba programme. In this the Al-Da'wa was assisted throughout by the 'education' outreach (*Al-Talim*) which was yet another tool and arguably the most effective method for influencing children. The educational curriculum was focused on the Islamic sciences, such as study of the Quran, rather than physics or mathematics. There is no instruction in secular subjects or in any technical skills, nor is there any formal schooling beyond the elementary level. Its core motivation is to train the next generation of soldiers, the actual citizenry of the caliphate in the making.

The registration officer and Moisin, the Escort, like all functionaries, saw the caliphate and its territories as a sovereign state educating its citizens. The caliphate was no longer a resurgence of a long-past idea, but a reality with a distinct and impressive geographical presence. When an idea is transformed into a physical entity, the chances are that it is here to stay.

The members of the group had now become the citizens of the Islamic State. The registration officer called the hostel manager to arrange the allocation of living quarters for them. Ameena, a portly matron of around fifty, scurried towards him.

'Have these citizens lodged in the eastern sector hostel,' he instructed her, adding, 'there is a large family so you may have to arrange a few rooms in immediate proximity to each other'. Ameena nodded her understanding. Married couples could stay together under a single roof but, apart from children and infants, men and women lived in separate rooms. Members of large families were given rooms close to each other.

Ameena started the business of identifying and dividing the citizens into small lots and allotting them quarters. These were noted on the forms which completed the initial packet of information which would be fed into the database.

The Escort rose, his job was done and he had to meet friends in the local police station. 'I will take your leave, Habibi,' he said to the registration officer.

'Yes, yes I will get this lot sorted out.' The officer was already engrossed in his duties. 'I will see you tomorrow at the mosque.' Both men waved goodbyes and the Escort walked out and got into his Toyota, dismissing his men for some sorely needed rest and instructing them to convene the next day at noon. The vehicles would have to be driven back to Turkey.

Moisin started his car and headed towards the town square police station in order to comply with its legal rulings. The Islamic State maintained a local police force in the Aleppo and Raqqa provinces. A provincial report for Aleppo released as early as June 2014 had made it amply clear that the main function of the police forces is to serve as the 'executive body for the court.' Additionally, the police forces are tasked with maintaining internal security through the deployment of regular patrols within towns.

The State had provided the local police patrols with dedicated vehicles and distinctive branded uniforms. They operated under the purview of a different jurisdiction than of the religious police, thus keeping administration and religion in tandem and yet disconnected in governance.

The Islamic State was significantly dependent on support from the Sunni tribes and had set up a bureau of public relations and tribal affairs within its provincial administration to deal with problems of security, property disputes, and the distribution of resources. In conjunction with the support of tribal elders, this went a long way in cementing ties and generating goodwill. Indeed, in December 2015, the group's English-language periodical, *Dabiq*, had published a detailed article regarding the Aleppo tribal outreach programme. The support of the tribes was required to capture and hold oil fields, water resources, dams (for both power and water), and key border towns to preserve supply routes, grain silos and cultivable land that produced wheat.

The Escort wanted to meet his friend Mustaq, who was the section-in-charge of the local tribal affairs department; there was the matter of his niece who had come of age, and Mustaq would help in finding a suitable marriage alliance.

Maldives

The office of the foreign affairs minister of Maldives is housed in the seven-storeyed new extension building in the Boduthakurufaanu area in Malé. If the sergeant of the police station's attitude was uncooperative, Sameer thought, then the officials in the foreign affairs ministry were positively unfriendly. The lady behind the protocol officer's desk spoke in short and impatient sentences.

'You went to the police? Then why are you here?'

'Well, since my relatives went abroad I… ' Sameer started to reply.

'We are not the police, if it's a police matter why are you here?'

Sameer said, 'I want to request the minister to confirm their whereabouts.'

'Why? Are they involved in an accident?'

'Not to my knowledge, but I fear that they may have gone to Syria for jihad.'

'Oh? Did they leave a note, or do you have any information?' The lady's voice was sharper now. 'Then this becomes a matter for internal security, I suggest you go to them. What do you expect the foreign affairs ministry to do? Do you have any proof that they went to Syria?

'Actually, no, I don't.' As Sameer spoke he realized how inadequately prepared he sounded; the impotence and the frustrations wrought by the last two days seemed to well up in bile, and suddenly, he wanted to reach over and shake the lady by the shoulders. *Look at me!* he wanted to scream. *I have lost all my siblings, I have lost my family, do you know that? Can you imagine how that feels? Look at me! Help me! Please*... but he took several deep breaths instead. 'Please,' he continued more calmly, 'just let me meet the minister and request him to trace my siblings—there are children involved, you see.' Sameer's eyes teared up and he was unable to continue.

For the first time, the lady officer's expression softened, her eyes ran over the distraught man sitting in front of her, a good-looking man, she thought, a doctor according to his papers, and obviously a man who cherished his family. *Allah*, she thought, *how it must feel!*

She said, gently this time, 'Look, Dr Ibraheem, I am just a junior official here so I can't really make any promises. Why don't you leave your petition here? I will give you a receipt and let's see what happens, okay? The honourable minister examines every petition. Okay? We will get back to you.'

Sameer nodded and asked for directions to the washrooms. By the time he returned she had processed his petition, it now lay in the in-tray. He thanked her and the official nodded, her eyes followed him as he left the office. The lady sat staring at her desk and then looked across the room at her colleague. Both women exchanged glances and shrugged; there would be much to chat about during lunch break.

Raqqa

As the Escort's car wound its way through the lanes of Raqqa the hostel manager, Ameena, finished allotting rooms to the group.

She had received special directions from the registration officer and had housed the young man named Aabir near the cleric's quarters. He had accepted the arrangement cheerfully enough and Ameena's usually stern face softened at the memory of the young man's face; he had such a nice smile, she thought; may Allah bless him and the others, she prayed; may they be followed by millions more.

Inside one of the rooms Munsiu and Zahi looked at each other. The last few days they had always been in a group, even at the hotel in Gaziantep. It was the first time in days that they had a private moment together. Outside, the wind made a low keening sound as it blew through the fronds of the date palms. Munsiu cleared his throat and was about to speak but Zahi preempted him.

'How could you?' she began, her voice trembling with emotion. 'You said we were going to Singapore for a vacation!' her voice rose. 'How could you do this? Bring me here on a false pretext... Here? For what? To die?

'Lower your voice,' Munsiu cautioned, 'the others may hear... '

'Did you know you were coming here when you married me? Did you?' Zahi continued unabated, her voice rising further, a note of hysteria creeping into it now. Munsiu advanced towards her and made to put his hands on her shoulders, to draw her close but Zahi batted his hands away.

'No!' Her voice was a scream now. 'Answer me... '

'Sssh! Lower your voice. *I said, lower your...* ' Munsiu hissed and grabbed her by the arms.

'No!' Zahi finally lost all vestige of control and pushed him away violently. Five seconds later, she lay sprawled on the ground, looking up in disbelief, no one had struck her in her life before, not her father or her mother… no one! Munsiu's open-handed slap had caught her squarely on her left cheekbone and had spun her to the right, and she had fallen. Now, as she propped herself on her elbow, she had but one thought in her mind, how could she have been so stupid... so blind?

An hour later Zahi watched her husband asleep on the bed, a forearm pillowing his head, and his mouth quivering every time he snored. He had held her close after that slap and had spoken about Islam and Sharia and how true values had deteriorated and that order and honour needed to be restored. He had spoken about how religious conviction was the supreme test of Islam. He had talked for a long time but she had been in a daze and uncomprehending. He had been unconvincing and above all, he hadn't been her Munsiu, her husband... This man was a stranger, she thought.

Zahi sat on the plastic chair and watched her husband for long minutes before she rose, her cheek throbbing with pain, walked across the room and picked up her handbag. The bathroom was tiny, about 2 metres by 3, with a squat toilet to the left and a shower that didn't work. The tap did, however, and as the water started pouring into the 20-gallon plastic bucket Zahi looked at the cell phone she had taken out of her handbag. She didn't know what made her not surrender that phone; she had given up her usual one. This one she had purchased in India when she visited five months ago. She had loaded it with the generic prepaid card sold in the airport at Mumbai and it had sort of remained with her as an 'extra'. She didn't know if it had any data or credit left or even if it would work here.

Zahi thought further, her first instinct was to call or text her parents but calling was risky and she feared using up whatever credit she had left. She did not have the English-to-Dwivehi language converter software on this instrument and her parents didn't follow English; in fact they rarely even bothered to check text messages. No, she thought, my best chance is to text Ahmed, my brother, because that's what my parents would do anyway if I were to contact them. They would call him.

She pressed on the power button and a moment later the phone made a tinkling sound that signified that it was booting up. The tinkle was eclipsed by the sound of the running water, Zahi held her breath, She opened the door a crack and peered into the room, her husband was still sleeping. She pulled the door shut gently and stared intently at the screen.

CHAPTER FIVE

United States

The two men continued to converse on the deck of the house in Albany, the sound of the flowing stream reaching their ears, a natural melody that ebbed and flowed with the air currents, and with the voices of the men in contrapuntal question and answer. Liyaqat Chowdhary had just put down a cup of coffee to reply to a query from his friend, and the Contact listened with undiminished attention, interjecting only now and then.

'But of course,' Liyaqat was saying, 'the Islamic State's Caliph and his senior leadership *is obviously* highly ideologically driven, which sets the tone when it comes to the policies and the vision for the future. So now let me approach the nature and content of the Islamic State's ideology because that has been lost in translation and grouped—rather erroneously—under the common head of everyday Islamic terrorism. We must learn to recognize the ocean of difference that lies between them.

'You must view the Islamic State's ideology on two overlapping planes. The first is *Jihadi-Salafism*, the school of Islamic political belief which the group advocates so vehemently, and the second is the Islamic State's extraordinary level of *hard-line orientation* within this school that, to a large degree, is what separates it from Al-Qaeda today. Notwithstanding this, my friend, I suspect—or rather, I fear—that in due course this hard line will also be toed by the members of Al-Qaeda, given the state of affairs anywhere around the globe today.'

The Scholar leaned back, his voice lower but somehow more intense. The Contact leaned forward… this had to be important.

'The term *Salafī* is said to derive from *al-salaf al-sālih*, meaning literally, 'the venerable ancestors of the first generations of Islam' whom the Salafist ideologues choose to emulate. In short, my friend, Salafism focuses on eliminating idolatry (*shirk*) and affirming God's Oneness (*tawhid*). These Salafis view themselves as the only true Muslims, considering those who practise 'idol worship' to be outside the tenets of the Islamic faith. Those worshipping, directly or indirectly, any idols, animal forms, saints, tombs, and so on, are considered apostates or those who have chosen to spurn the religion. These include the Shia and worse…' Liyaqat paused for effect and concluded in a sibilant whisper, '… those participating in a democratic system of government!'

The Contact raised his eyebrows at the Scholar who nodded in rueful confirmation. 'The Shia are considered guilty of *shirk* on account of their excessive reverence of the Prophet Mohammed's family among other things, while democrats err in assigning 'representatives' to God in matters of legislation which is deemed to be the prerogative of the Divine Legislators alone. 'Now,' said

Liyaqat, 'Jihadi-Salafism is a distinct school of thought in Sunni Islam. It encompasses an international network of religious authoritarians, thought-change leaders, websites, media outlets, and more importantly, countless supporters on social media. Their religious tenets emanate from an extremist, myopic and limited reading of Islamic scripture, one that is also textually uncompromising and enmeshed in a pre-modern theological tradition that has been through the last several decades extensively elaborated on by newer and newer cadres of religious authorities.'

'So,' the Scholar continued, 'the first impression one comes away with from this school of thought is that there is no distinction between religion and state. All decisions are based on a hard-line interpretation of the Islamic law, which is brutally enforced in the areas controlled by the Islamic State'. The Contact nodded grimly and made a note in his pad.

Liyaqat's thin lips stretched into another of his ironic smiles. 'Funnily enough,' he mused, 'their ideology is almost exactly the same as that of other groups such as the Al-Qaeda and the Taliban. The only thing that differentiates the Islamic State from the rest of the pack is the urgency in its approach to timing and the conditions it finds necessary to establish a caliphate.'

'Which other groups differ from them in these areas?' asked the Contact curiously.

'A name that comes to mind is Jabhat al-Nusra,' said Liaqat promptly. 'The al-Nusra front, which serves as the Al-Qaeda's official affiliate in the Syrian Civil War, believe that although the long-term goal is to establish an Islamic caliphate, the time is not yet right for it.' Liyaqat paused and shook his head. 'But in the end, they all want the same thing: a dominant Islam with zero tolerance of all other religious faiths.'

'What drives the typical Salafist today?' The Contact was keen to know what they were conceptually up against.

'Ideology,' replied Liaqat succinctly. 'Salafist ideology has evolved out of the idea of a return to the supposedly pure form of Islam practised by the immediate successors to the founder of Islam, Prophet, and the earliest Muslims. This school of thought rejects any later additions, such as *bid'ah* (innovation), as un-Islamic. As a result, the doctrine allows its practitioners to declare as *takfir* (heretics) all other Muslims who deviate from this strictly defined interpretation of Islam.

'Sayyid Qutb, the Muslim Brotherhood ideologue hanged by Egyptian President Gamal Abdel Nasser in 1966, was also a major influence on all Jihadist groups, the Islamic State being no exception. Qutb's contribution to jihadist ideology was to accentuate the idea of *jahiliyya*, which believes that Arabs were in a state of ignorance prior to the appearance of Prophet and his Islamic teachings. Qutb termed anything other than strict adherence to Sharia law and Islam as *jahiliyya*, including all other contemporary Muslim regimes and schools of thought. He then advocated the violent overthrow of all such regimes in order to replace them with an Islamic state. These ideas were further developed by the thinkers and jihadists that would go on to form Al-Qaeda, prominent amongst them being Abdullah Azzam, the so-called father of global jihadism and Osama bin Laden.'

Liyaqat found his legs cramping. Unable to sit still any longer, he rose from his chair and paced the deck with his hands clasped behind his back. The Contact's eyes and ears followed his movements, not wanting to miss a word of the Scholar's insight.

'Now that I have mentioned the Muslim Brotherhood, let me now introduce it as a causal factor at this stage. The Muslim Brotherhood that was founded in Egypt in 1928 by Hasan al-Banna, as a political movement bent on winning power and influence in society and capturing the state, was and remains an exclusively Sunni movement, but it is not implacably hostile to other Islamic sects, such as Shia Islam, or other orientations such as Sufi mysticism. This movement had emerged as a response to the perceived rise of Western imperialism and the associated decline of Islam as a way of life. The Brotherhood therefore sought to reverse these trends via grassroots Islamic activism.'

Abruptly Liyaqat stopped and turned around, his eyes meeting those of the Contact's.

'Am I clear or have I confused you, my solivagant friend?' the Scholar asked, his eyes twinkling. 'You don't mind me decribing you in such words do you?'

The Contact was rarely discomposed and he had to admit, if only to himself, that Liyaqat's words had struck a chord inside him somewhere. I forget, he thought, this is an extremely intelligent and perceptive man. I have approached him less than five times and already he knows that I am one of those that stare with dread into an abyss of their own making.

He maintained eye contact with Liyaqat and replied, 'No, I am on board as of now,' and waved his notebook in emphasis, A slow nod of understanding was exchanged, and Liyaqat continued his story.

'The Muslim Brotherhood espoused the restoration of the caliphate as the ideal system of government for the Islamic world. Consequent to the defeat and dissolution of the Ottoman Caliphate in 1924 after the Turkish war of independence via a motion passed by the Grand National Assembly of Turkey. They clamoured for the reestablishment of the caliphate.'

'In the later decades of the 20th century the Arab Middle East saw the rise of violent Islamist groups influenced by both Muslim Brotherhood activism and Salafi exclusivist activity. These groups, including the Egyptian Islamic Jihad, the Islamic Group, the Armed Islamic Group and the Salafi Group for Preaching and Combat in Algeria, were the forerunners of today's Jihadi-Salafi groups. These groups aimed to overthrow the established governments and replace them with Islamic states. Although Al-Qaeda shared a similar ideology, the group advocated a different strategy, focusing on attacking the United States as the first step to creating an Islamic state in the Middle East. Their leader, Osama bin Laden, spoke frequently of restoring the caliphate'.

The Scholar stopped pacing and returned to his chair. 'Let's take a break,' Liyaqat suggested. 'And now's a good time to dig into some of that excellent biryani that you so kindly brought.' The Contact grinned at his mentor's obvious appetite and both men moved to the dining room. A 10-minute wait resulted in two plates heaped with fragrant biryani. The Contact looked across the table at Liyaqat. The man was clearly enjoying his lunch with no intention of resuming his monologue until his hunger was satiated. The Contact similarly directed his attention to the meal. Later, both men repaired, satisfied, to the living room. It had grown too hot to sit outside.

The Contact waited expectantly for Liyaqat to continue. The Scholar slipped comfortably back into his narrative as if he'd never broken off. 'In conjunction with the rise of these groups,' he said, 'or rather, as some say, as a consequence of it, there formed a loosely knit network of independent scholars and mullahs that gave ideological emphasis to the emergent jihadi movement. The works of scholars such as the Palestinian Abu Muhammad al-Maqdisi, and the Syrian Abu Basir al-Tartusi, helped set the tone in the sense that their focus on the more violent aspects of Salafism gave birth to Jihadi-Salafism. In the last quarter century, jihadism has thus been increasingly dominated by its Salafi dimension. Naturally, a byproduct of this was that the

Muslim Brotherhood authors, who according to Salafis do not adhere to proper theology, are seldom quoted or referenced by modern jihadis. Rather, works by Ibn Taymiyya and the others of the Wahhabi tradition became the ideological backbone of the movement.'

'If jihadism were to be viewed as a political paradigm then the Al-Qaeda would be its left and the Islamic State its right. In principle, both organizations adhere to Salafism and aspire to be the face of Salafi Jihadism. But the Islamic State does so with greater aggression, when compared with Al-Qaeda. It is absolutely uncompromising on doctrinal matters and promotes an unforgiving version of Salafi thought. Most Islamic State official publications are little more than long quotations from Wahhabi scholars, but they are aesthetically presented—which might explain some of their appeal. Have you seen any copies of the *Dabiq*?'

The Contact nodded, he had looked up and found most editions of the Islamic State's online publication. The *Dabiq* was glossy and obviously brought out by tech- and design-savvy persons, bearing all the hallmarks of a world-class electronic publication. The images were high-definition, the narrative and ideological content persuasive, the pages beautifully executed and visually arresting—pretty much the *Vogue* of Islamic publications.

'Well,' Liyaqat said, clearly winding down, 'last but not the least, my friend, it is noteworthy that the Islamic State's "jihad" is directed mainly against the region's Shia community. Apart from the differences in ideology, the IS perceives that the Shia have ambitions of expansion in the Middle East and this necessitates fighting them. The IS believes that the Shia want a "Shi'ite crescent" extending from Tehran to Beirut, and that the Islamic Republic of Iran, the Hezbollah in Lebanon, and the Asad regime in Syria, all form part of this "crescent". They are convinced that Iran's leaders are aiming to "turn Iraq into a Shi'ite state", and that the United States is complicit in their plan. According to the IS, Iraq's recent historical transition from a Sunni to a Shia majority is evidence of an imminent "Shi'itization".'

An hour later, the Contact was on his way back. It was only late afternoon and he was confident that he would beat the evening commuter traffic and reach home in good time. As he drove he ruminated over the Scholar's briefing, it was worth every dollar he had placed in the envelope that he had handed to him, and more. No doubt the Scholar would in the future call upon him for a small 'favour' and the Contact would gladly oblige. It was an understanding they had, and both men profited from it.

Once he had exited the driveway of Liyaqat Chowdhary's house he had stopped and checked his email and found the names and photographs of the family in the inbox. The Contact had then made a call before he drove on further. It had been a brief one and he had forwarded the photographs of the male members to someone he knew in Bengaluru in

India (the women were sure to be wearing hijabs and identification would have been near impossible). He had added the flight details and the bit about the infant and child. The instructions were to find out any and every findable fact with regard to their place of stay, purchases, local contacts if any, and the CCTV footage from the airport and other areas. The person he called was an ex-police officer, intelligent, resourceful, and above all, dependable. He could be trusted to keep his mouth shut. If he came up with vital info then there would naturally be a bonus, else, he would draw the usual 5,000 Indian rupees for an eight-hour day fee, plus expenses.

Malé

Ahmed Idris was in his study after a tiring day at work. Tiring because of the increased effort required to maintain focus and composure. The bottle of Grey Goose stood half empty on the desk, the last two cubes of ice in the teal-coloured ceramic bowl floated in a shallow pool of water. His cell phone beeped. He couldn't read it from where he was as he had plugged it in for charging a few feet away. Idris rose and walked around his desk to pick up his phone. The icon signalled a text message and from an unfamiliar number. Idris frowned. Text messages were rare, everyone communicated by Whatsapp or Twitter or Facebook these days, and the number was unfamiliar. His right thumb touched the icon.

Moments later Ahmed Idris sagged as if he had been kicked in the belly. His legs carried him to the small sofa and he slumped into it as he continued staring with disbelief at the words on the screen:

'Dear brother, Munsiu and the others tricked me, I am in Raqqa, very low on credit, this is my India number, so won't be able to text more than a few times. I am at a hostel run by a woman called Ameena, it's a yellow building with palm trees on one side and the street on the other, Please get me out of here. Zahi.'

Ahmed Idris read the message a third time. Of course, he thought, this was the number Zahi had used in India last year. She had purchased one of those ultra-slim phones that were in vogue at the time. He remembered laughing at the pink 'hello kitty' cover she had got for it, the one with the white dangler swinging below. So! Idris thought, as he took a deep breath, after all these months the phone was still with her. His mind whirled with the implications but he restrained himself from instantly tapping out a reply. Instead, dialled the US number that the Contact had given him.

The Contact would know what to do next.

CHAPTER SIX

The Contact was cleaning the cage when Idris's call came through. Inside the cage, two parakeets scattered more birdseed than they ate, and seemed to have an inexhaustible supply of feathers to discard. The parakeets were short-term guests; their owner was in the Bahamas on a week-long vacation and had requested the Contact to house them. It was the fourth day and he was already looking forward to their departure. They chirped incessantly and had squawking matches several times a day. The dog had peered at them for several long moments on the first day, subjected them to a few disdainful sniffs and thereafter proceeded to ignore them altogether.

The Contact picked up the cell phone; he noticed that there was also a message delivery notification.

'Hello,' he spoke into the phone.

Idris's voice came over instantly, clearly excited. 'I just got a message from my sister, Zahi, she is in Syria. I have forwarded her message to you. Take a look at it.'

'Oh? Wait a minute,' the Contact replied. Scanning his apps, he clicked on the message. He read it twice, his mind racing with the implications it held.

'What type of card is she using? What's the number?'

'It's an India number,' Idris replied. 'She had bought it in Mumbai a few months ago when she went there for a couple of weeks. It's a prepaid, perhaps, with a couple of hundred rupees of credit left in it. It must have caught a local signal over there.'

The Contact rapidly assessed the development before he spoke. 'Okay, first and foremost make sure you have someone go to a Mumbai outlet and put two or three thousand rupees' worth of credit into that SIM. That way she can keep communicating. Then, send her a message telling her that you are arranging her return. Tell her to only use the phone after 11pm at night and never for more than three minutes. Ask her if she has a charging cable for the phone, if not, then we are going to be severely limited in communications. She is to contact nobody else, not even her mother—make that very clear. Tell her that her life depends on it.'

The Contact barely paused for breath before the next sentence. 'You can't tell anyone either, certainly not Sameer, you understand? Idris replied in the affirmative, he had heard that persons who left on jihad kept intermittent telephone contact with their families. Should one of Sameer's siblings give him a call and should Sameer make the slightest mention about Zahi's message... Idris shuddered at the thought of what would ensue and the inevitable severance of this slender lifeline. No, the Contact was right; he couldn't afford to say anything to anyone about this, not even to his wife.

The Contact's voice went on snapping out instructions. 'I want you to tell her to send you photographs of the building she is staying in and of any landmarks nearby, especially street names or monuments, statues and the like. Tell her to be extremely careful and take no chances. Even if it means several days, absolutely no risks should be taken, stress that. Wait! Actually, on second thought, tell her to note down the street names and building numbers and text them as soon as she can.'

The curt, rapidfire orders went on: 'You have that other number yet? The one I told you to get?'

'Yes,' Idris replied, 'I got it this evening, I was going to tell you that.'

'Great, give her that number and tell her not to text you anymore on your usual one. Send it to me, too. From now on, we use only that number.'

The Contact suddenly grew silent. He hated what he had to say next and it was a while before he could bring himself to say it. 'Idris, my friend, you know what this means now, don't you?'

At the other end Ahmed Idris's brow furrowed in puzzlement. 'I… er… don't follow you, what do you mean?' he asked.

'Your sister is the only one coming out, voluntarily I mean,' the Contact hesitated again, and Idris's eyes widened as realization hit him; he felt cold inside.

The Contact continued: 'The others can't be saved, not even the little girl, nor the infant. You have to come to terms with that and the Sameer situation, you understand?'

Ahmed Idris stared as if hypnotized at the paperweight on his desk and his stomach balled up painfully They would have to string Sameer along, he realized, they would have to lie and keep lying all the time pretending to help him if they were to have any chance at all of getting Zahi out. Every inch of him shrank at the prospect of such… he couldn't think of the right word… chicanery? Allah! he thought, how has it come to this? Idris composed himself with an effort. He wouldn't dwell on it now, now was not the time. He spoke into the phone calmly, 'I understand, my friend; I leave it to you… just, just get my sister out.'

The Contact had to keep a grip on his own voice when he heard the resolve in his friend's, but he had one last order: 'There is one more thing. As soon as you can, that is, within the next couple of days, I want you to go to the house where Zahi used to stay and take a couple of pictures of yourself with the house in the background and one of her room.'

At the other end of the line, Idris nodded, even though the reason for the latest instruction eluded him. No doubt his friend knew what he was doing. 'Expect a call from Sameer,' he told the Contact before ending the call. 'Apparently he has received some news from the bank.'

The Contact finished cleaning the cage and soaped the ammonia-laced smell of bird-shit off his hands. I am going pop a bottle of Krystal the day these birds leave, he promised himself wryly.

The phone rang again. That would be Sameer, he thought, as he walked towards his desk.

It was indeed Sameer, and after the initial

awkwardness of self-introductions, he spoke unhurriedly, and the Contact was struck by the soft and well-modulated voice of the doctor from Maldives.

'I went to the Bank in Malé,' Sameer cleared his throat and began, clearly ill at ease with the nature of the conversation and the discomfiture of having to speak to a stranger.

The Contact understood his hesitation. 'I know that it's not an everyday situation and a normal conversation for you,' he said reassuringly. 'You can ask Ahmed and he will tell you that I have had some experience in these sort of matters and besides, I am a family friend, I will help in every way I can. So please tell me everything.'

After a couple of seconds, Sameer's voice returned over the line. 'Yes, I know you are Ahmed's friend and I don't have anyone else who could possibly help me with this thing, so... yes, the bank manager told me that between them my family had over the last 15 days made a number of withdrawals amounting to a total of approximately 65,000 in US dollars. They weren't able to access the fixed deposits as my parents' consent and signatures were required.'

Sameer continued, 'They did however clear out the contents of the lockers. There was a whole lot of jewellery and gold there—I can't even begin to make an estimate of those.'

The Contact considered this additional piece of information. The cash alone, he thought to himself, was a huge amount considering where the group had gone. In Syria the merest whiff of gold or cash would attract its own brand of cutthroats. 'Did you ask the manager about any recent ATM activity by any of your family members?' he asked Sameer.

'Yes,' Sameer replied, 'I was about to come to that. My sister Zoona, and Munsiu, my brother, used their credit cards to make small purchases in a place called Gaziantep in Turkey. According to the bank official this was two days ago'.

'Oh?' observed the Contact. 'Well, that's news. It gives us a location.They probably plan to meet someone who will take them across the border either to Syria or Iraq,' he surmised.

'Yes, you are right,' Sameer said. He hadn't thought about Iraq or, for that matter, Libya. Sameer had been surfing the Internet for information and news articles on ISIS. Some of the things he had read had astonished him. That means they could be anywhere. He spoke into the phone. 'Do you know someone there?'

'I know a few people,' replied the Contact 'I have sources, let me try and find out what I can. I need you to do something in the meantime. I want you to prepare a brief note on each family member, details like education, special skills, hobbies, any medical history etc.'

'Yes, Ahmed told me about the medical thing, I will send you notes, although I may have to ask my parents for some details. Is that okay?'

'I would prefer if you didn't ask them,' replied the Contact. 'Just send me what you can find out on your own. Also email me copies of the petition and complaint that you filed at the police station and the ministry of foreign affairs'

'I'll do that right away,' said Sameer.

'Any luck with the call detail records of their phones?' the Contact asked.

'No,' replied Sameer, 'they refused to give them to me, they said that the police had directed them not to disclose any information as it's an ongoing investigation.'

Sameer's voice lowered as he admitted, 'Today I was followed by two people. I pointed them out to a friend and he informed me that they belong to a local gang here called Kuredhinvaaru. They were outside the ministry building and I saw them again when I left the bank. They were on a motorcycle.'

The Contact pondered this for a moment; he knew that gang-related violence was an increasingly common phenomenon in recent years in the Maldives and the nature of violence had grown more brutal with the advent and rapid increase of drug-trafficking. There were around 25 different gangs operating in Malé alone, with a membership numbering anywhere between fifty to a couple of hundred. The situation was more of a social anxiety than an officially recognized law-and-order issue because of the political-criminal nexus, and the escalating level of violence being a matter of concern even to the gang members themselves. Businesses and neighbourhoods were invariably affected and property damage was the inevitable side-effect.

Gangs generally had patrons with political and business interests who employed them to achieve their aims, and naturally, joining the membership of a gang had become an easy path for youth seeking to earn money in an environment where jobs were scarce and the path to legitimate employment difficult. The police and judiciary were perceived to be exacerbating the problems by handing out harsh sentences and creating criminal records for minor offences. The Maldives law allowed employers to access existing police records of job applicants. Even a brief police detention meant that the person acquired a police record which would last for up to five years.

Most gang members had either never been employed or were currently unemployed for an extended period. The unemployment issue was of such severity that in some areas those who peddled drugs considered themselves employed. A good percentage of gang members used as well as sold drugs. Having being arrested and detained 'boosted' one's image within the gang and key members were often back on the streets after being charged, with the release being arranged under parole, presidential pardon or under the 'Second Chance' programme.

Each gang took pride on its members having better bikes, flashier jewellery, more mobile phones, electronic accessories and designer clothing, perhaps even a car. The quality and quantity of such trappings were the badges of the gang's eminence.

The Contact was aware that there was a reciprocal relationship between gang members and politicians and businessmen; cash and easy access to drugs and alcohol as payment for services rendered with the amount payable known only to the gang leader. Female members were put to work as 'honey-traps' for political or business opponents to fall into, and to make video tapes that were used as leverage. Sometimes, women members were then used as outright prostitutes for additional income.

The Contact spoke into the phone again. 'I think they are just watching your activities and do not intend to harm you. But be careful and avoid walking in dark or isolated areas, stick to populated public places and don't approach or confront strangers who may come up to you. In fact, from now on I would recommend that you avoid being out after dark altogether.'

'I understand,' Sameer said quietly. 'So there is no clue or information about them?' he asked, anguish evident in his voice. 'I know it's very early to ask you but...' his voice tapered away.

'Yes, it is still early days yet,' the Contact said in a reassuring tone, 'but your information has given me something to work on. Don't worry, I am confident that we will make progress. Sometimes, things take shape quickly and sometimes, it's a long frustrating process before progress is made and an operation can be mounted. The thing to do is to keep chipping away at it.'

The Contact disconnected the phone, he suddenly felt a sour taste in his mouth. It hasn't been three days yet, he thought, and already the lying and deceit has begun. He walked back to his desk and studied the laptop screen. For days, he had been surfing the website of the One World Group.

Within hours of receiving the call from his friend three days earlier, the Contact had realized that sooner rather than later the range and nature of his activities would place him under the scanner of a whole multitude of agencies on both sides of the globe. Further, he was acutely aware that he would require the assistance of some of them, it would be quid pro quo—it had to be, the Contact reflected—these days, there were no free lunches. Or, as an old British acquaintance of his used to say, 'I'm afraid you'll have to sing for your supper, old boy'. He would have to not only create a sense of legitimacy but in addition, leave an inerasable trail of his intentions in case he was called upon to explain his actions by the laws that be. For that he had searched the options and decided upon the One World Group.

The Group was the brain child of Abid Rustom, who became its Chief Executive Officer. Abid was a former FBI Supervisory Special Agent who was one of the few people in the agency post 9/11 that understood and spoke Arabic with any fluency. Talk about being in the right place at the right time! the Contact reflected. Abid had been worth his weight in gold and had been vital in investigating and supervising the most sensitive cases of terrorrism, indeed he had been privy to the most secret and sensitive details, including the East Africa Embassy bombings, the attack on the US naval ship, and the events surrounding 9/11. Today Rustom served as a member of the Homeland Security Advisory Council in the US.

Abid established the One World Group with the intention of optimizing on the talent, reach and experience of a coterie of international experts in security, law enforcement, military strategy and terrorism to cater to the maze of intertwining issues when it came to handling global security today. The Group was headquartered in New York and had regional offices in London, Dubai, and Hong Kong, as well as operations in the Americas, Europe, the Middle East, Asia, and Africa. Abid Rustom's team provided customized services to governments and multinational organizations. The Contact regularly read their publications and had come to appreciate the depth and detail of their investigations. He looked for and found the telephone number of their New York office and dialed it. Twenty minutes later, after a conversation with an obviously intelligent but cautious official, he had an email address. The Contact began to type an email, stopping frequently to refer to a bunch of papers that served as notes. An hour later he clicked on 'send' and then powered off. He didn't expect a reply for several hours.

CHAPTER SEVEN

The tent had been put up on a grassy knoll with a view of the waterline and about 50 metres away from the dense clumps of buckthorn shrub. It was a large one, 18 feet by 18 feet with a ceiling height of 11 feet. It was semi-rigid and had an air-conditioner duct piped into it. A fuel-fed generator growled continually outside. It was the kind of general-purpose modular tent used by expeditions and armed forces the world over. This one had found its way from the US army surplus stores through a myriad dealers and contractors and had ultimately landed in Syria via a ransacked military warehouse in Iraq. The interior housed a couple of collapsible metal tables, chairs and a bed. There was a small refrigerator but the bulk of the space was taken up by a wide assortment of metal trunks and what was obviously photo and film equipment, including a row of charging points. A man stood by one of the tables peering at a large writing pad. He wore a white shirt and desert camouflage-patterned trousers. An oversized floppy hat with a wide brim lay on the table. It was close to dawn but there was no hint of wind and the air was heavy with humidity. The man's white shirt was already spotted with damp patches of sweat and the rolled-up canvas flaps that served as the door hung limply at either end.

Abu Nasser al Beljaki, moviemaker for the IS, squinted down at the days' shooting schedule. There was the child warriors' documentary to be completed over the next two weeks and he had reserved a two-hour slot in the late afternoon for that. The mosque, 15 kilometres away, had a large courtyard where the martial arts training sequence was to be filmed; he had inspected the indoor set for that the day before and had come away satisfied. The execution shoot was well into its initial stages and right now they were waiting for the sun to rise by a few more degrees so that the light came in at exactly the correct angle so as to frame the soldier's head and features in a suitably 'ethereal' halo. The group that would enact the final execution scene were all good-looking young men with a 'pirate-turned-priest' air about them and with just a hint of the 'bad boy' still discernable. Just the type, the Moviemaker thought, to attract those impressionable young girls, the prospective jihadi brides.

Then he had to do a clip for the 'Life in the Khilafat' series which was an ongoing project of his. The clip would have to be edited, dubbed and then added to the main storyline, a task that would take hours in the studio. A full day's work lay ahead—and now this last-minute addition by his seniors. A specialty item for the archives, to be pulled out of the cloud-based databank and released at the appropriate moment. The Moviemaker had done these specialty items many times before, they were part of a brilliantly drawn-out strategy of the IS that allowed it to claim responsibility for successful operations against the Kuffar whilst demonstrating planning, premeditation and coordination on its part. A majorly successful public relations and outreach exercise, the kind any multinational would grandly and be proud of.

He glanced across at the slim figure in the uniform sitting on one of the chairs in the tent. The youngster seemed fascinated by the preparations in progress, his wide eyes darting from one activity to another. He had obviously never viewed or participated in a shoot before and his face was alight with curiosity and delight in equal parts. The Moviemaker smiled involuntarily as their eyes met. Charming guy, he thought again.

The IS Moviemaker was a broad shouldered man of 5'10", and long hair that ended with turned-in curls falling to his shoulders. The low forehead and bushy eyebrows ensured that he narrowly missed being a handsome man, nevertheless he made a striking figure as he strode out of the tent giving directions in a deep voice audible at a range of 300 yards—which was precisely the distance from the ridge over which the young and charismatic fighters would come running. With the grace of Allah their figures would be outlined by the rising sun. The Moviemaker wanted to draw a visual parallel between the dawn and the line of men carrying the IS flag. Good cinema, he knew, consisted of a clearly understood yet unspoken message. He had learned his trade in half a dozen places, including California, and had once indeed been the quintessential film neophyte doting on Spike Lee and Robert Rodriguez and others of their ilk. He then experimented with guerrilla filmmaking, and the lessons learnt there had been put to good use here, using low budgets, skeleton crews and simple props—sometimes even cooking up a scene or sequence on existing assets only.

The Islamic State had established a new propaganda wing called the al-Hayat Media Centre and the Moviemaker was a senior functionary. He had a very decent budget to go with, and a 15 or 20-minute video prepared by him cost anywhere between 125,000 to 150,000 US dollars, if one took into account the sophistication of the editing equipment required and the quality of the multiple HD cameras needed to produce a slick and professional piece of propaganda. Over the last few years, the use of video production as a weapon by extremist terror groups had become far more prevalent. The Islamic State in particular had made extensive use of produced video to multiply the impact of its agenda by leveraging its use of film cameras, public-relation savviness and social media to extend the reach of its message and doctrine globally. The Moviemaker knew that he wielded a weapon that rivalled in potency anything the Islamic State military possessed.

He glanced at the boy again. The youngster was inquisitively inspecting the array of chargers.

'So?' The Moviemaker spoke in English, 'How do you like our little set up here?'

The boy automatically flashed a smile at him and replied in what the Moviemaker instantly recognized was an American accent, 'Oh yeah, this is, like, so terrific, man, you guys got state-of-the-art here.'

'Oh? So you do some photography yourself?' queried the Moviemaker.

'Not much, some… I have a Canon 760D and fool around with it sometimes.'

The Moviemaker raised his heavy eyebrows. The Canon 760d was a serious piece of equipment. Not only was it expensive, it was used by professionals who wanted optimal results. So either this was a rich young man with the money to buy high-end kit or this guy knew what he was doing. On the other hand, considering what he knew of the young man, it was hardly surprising to find a desire to excel matched with an obvious aptitude for precision-technology. He had not failed to note that the boy maintained eye contact whenever he spoke and there was a decisive tone to his speech.

The Moviemaker abruptly turned away and went across to the entrance of the tent, pretending to look out. He was ever aware that his job description included being a chronicler for the dead and the soon-to-be-dead. The nature and theme of the boy's shoot hadn't escaped him and he did not want another razor-edged snapshot superimposed on his memory.

In the late '90s and early 2000s, terrorist groups experimented with and touted poorly recorded single-camera videos featuring long lectures, usually with scratchy audio and unclear grainy backgrounds. Now, the Islamic State Moviemaker and his production units were churning out documentaries, event coverage-like executions and also 'Mujatweets' which were single-minute or 30-second clips that highlighted life in the Islamic State. These mainly featured uniformed warriors playing with angel-faced toddlers, shops filled with brightly-coloured fruit and agro-produce and devout prayers at the mosque, basically playing up the joyous domestic aspect of life within the Islamic State. Not only were the videos more sophisticated than the ones produced by other Islamist groups, they were many more of them, and they came out faster. More importantly, the Islamic State gave licence to individuals to produce videos independently and propagate them at will. However, recruits around the world are expected to adhere to strict Sharia standards, censorship is by way of reprimands from other followers if any content is found objectionable or incorrect in projecting of the Islamic State's narrative. As a public relation strategy it was unstoppable, especially when compared with that of the Al-Qaeda, which issued a propaganda statement maybe once every month. The Moviemaker took pride in the speedy delivery rate his team had been consistently achieving; it wasn't surprising that they released video clips within hours of a conquest or operation. It was the immediacy of the information and its authentication by way of film media that made it the success it was.

The Islamic State had capitalized on the strengths and all-pervasiveness of social media from its very onset. From the relatively amateurish footage of the Al

Zarqawi-propagated execution videos, and the shock results those produced, the Islamic State had constantly innovated and adapted by using Facebook and Twitter and then elevating its tactics via peer-to-peer applications such as Telegram, Instagram, Surespot and lately, Trillion. They had exploited content-sharing on JustPaste.it and eventually decentralized its media operations, thereby allowing it to spread like a modern hydra with autonomous production units functioning from West Africa to as far as the Caucasus. The Islamic State was now adept at marketing, and was targetting a specific demographic—those waiting to be influenced by its message, anyhow, anytime, anywhere in the world.

The Moviemaker jerked to attention as the handheld walkie talkie radio on the desk crackled to life. The voice of his assistant came over the air: 'Sunrise in 10 minutes, Sir.'

'Right, I'm on my way,' the Moviemaker replied. He walked out of the tent towards the waterline where the team waited, his cameramen already sitting on the dollies. Ten minutes later, the line of men came over the skyline and the cameras started rolling.

The line advanced slowly, as practised in the rehearsals, but with a greater sense of purpose. The orange-suited prisoner stood out, partly because of the colour contrast and partly because of his bemused look and unkempt appearance. The prisoner shuffled rather than walked, his hands bound behind him, and his whole manner listless. He was bewildered by the numerous rehearsals and mock executions over the last couple of weeks and was now inured to the point of uncomprehending compliance, which was exactly what the Moviemaker desired. You could saw a man's head off but only once, and if he expected it, then the resultant panicked resistance, screaming and thrashing would mean blurred and partially blocked shots, in short, bad cinema. The Moviemaker prided himself on his art. His mandate was to produce films that would horrify the nonbelievers, fascinate those that had a taste for violence and the macabre, and, in its own puritanical way, attract those already converted. It was a fine line—but the Islamic State's chief Moviemaker trod it well.

The line stopped about 50 feet from the waterline, and the advancing men made an impressive picture in their tailored uniforms and with their rakish good looks. The Moviemaker signalled for a sideways pan of the left camera so as to get the profiles outlined against the breaking dawn. (This would be worked on later in the studio with the appropriate filters and music, to give the desired impression of a youthful army and indicating resolve and dedication, a sign of the future to come—as inevitable as the rising sun.) The cameras settled front and centre and the prisoner was made to kneel, his executioner behind him. They had already filmed and canned the executioner's speech the week before—over more than a dozen takes—much to the chagrin of the Moviemaker, the guy kept flubbing his lines and ultimately they had settled for a voice-over with the executioner miming the part. The prisoner was made to bend forward to a degree that didn't allow him any scope for lateral movement, and the executioner placed his left knee on the prisoner's back while his right hand slipped a broad-bladed hunting knife with the serrated edge against the left side of the prisoner's neck. His left hand had grabbed a bunch of hair and pulled back, the prisoners face turned upwards as the viens on his neck distended. 'Cut!,' the Moviemaker snapped and the executioner let go of the prisoner and stood up. The line of uniforms visibly relaxed. The prisoner straightened up mutely but remained on his knees. He was growing accustomed to the routine. The Moviemaker nodded in satisfaction, it was a wrap. The line disintegrated in seconds, the men spread themselves on the beach, and within minutes the catering unit rolled up with coffee and breakfast. It was bread and kebabs today, with small cups of curds on the side. The prisoner was also sitting next to his minders, hands free now, and eating as heartily as the rest of the team. The Moviemaker watched him with the intensity of one who recorded for posterity. He knew the next shoot would be the prisoner's last, the head placed upright between the shoulder blades, a long shot zooming in on to the features with the eyes half-open, rapidly dulling with the opaque glare of death. To the Moviemaker that was the intent, the message, the very threat of annihilation combined with the vision of a new world for the viewer.

A half-hour later the Moviemaker was back in the tent, the promise of a cooler day blowing in with the gusts of wind that made the door flaps dance. He looked up as Arshad entered, the ever-present iPad in hand. Arshad was the scriptwriter, the only person whom Beljaki could tolerate physically near him. The man said little apart from what his work demanded and always had the half-crouch of someone who expected to be kicked any second. We are both wounded animals, the Moviemaker thinks, and for a infinitesimal moment, his mind arched backward to an unspeakably painful past, his abdomen and buttocks racked by a momentary spasm. He shrugged off the memory with an ability born of sheer practice.

'As-salaam-walaikum, are we okay for today my friend?' he asked the scriptwriter.

'Wa alaikum as salaam, yes,' Arshad replied, his eyes meeting the Moviemaker who stared back as he reached for the schedule sheet and then broke eye contact as he tilted his head downward.

'I came for the add-on,' Arshad continued as he settled himself directly opposite the Moviemaker who looked up meeting the scriptwriter's eyes again.

'Yes,' said Beljaki, after a swallow. A measure of resolve added texture to his voice as he said, 'It's a small clip... perhaps three minutes'.

Both men leaned forward and discussed the last-minute addition to the days' schedule, the scriptwriter jotting down the occasional note. It would be the usual: a 2-minute affirmation to the Islamic State and its ideology with a mention of parents and the place of his origin, followed by a few clips showing the uniformed lad with a headband, the IS flag and finally with the prop. The scriptwriter had done this many times before and it was a half-hour job at best. He already had the bio-sheet and they slated it for noon, just before lunch. For the next few hours it would be the work-in-action 'Life in the Khilafat' series with today's shoot focused on the vegetable markets in the wilayats. The details having been worked out, both men went about their respective tasks, and the studio resumed work, as, in all businesses in the Islamic State too, output was everything.

The prop stood in the midday sun, its metal gleaming and the light bouncing off the glass in a dizzying sunburst. It wasn't possible to take the boy to the real thing because of the time factor but the prop was as good. It was basically a cutout of the original and could be reused if required. The boy was still in his uniform, they had done the initial bit with the speech and swearing of allegiance and another sound byte of him sitting under a tree with 'friends' having a meal. That sort of thing always looked good as it signified camaraderie, teamwork and so forth. This was the last bit and soon they would be done. The Moviemaker checked the wheeled ladder placed against the prop and was satisfied that it was secured with the chocks in place. He called out to the team and made adjustments to the board reflectors; there was a bit too much sunlight and he wanted to reduce the glare. This last scene was important and he wanted to use it for a fadeout. The Moviemaker looked at the set one final time and then called out for action.

The uniformed boy walked to the prop and paused at the ladder, he looked back for a second before climbing the ladder, at the top he swung his legs inside the narrow space with the easy agility of youth and looked to his left like he had been told to and smiled. The effect was startling, just the way the Moviemaker had imagined it would be. He grinned back; yes this was definitely one of his best. The boy raised his right hand high with the fingers clenched into a fist and that was it, cut and wrap. The boy would be taken back once he deposited the uniform with the costumes department and the sawn-off nose cone and cockpit that made up the prop would be towed back to the warehouse. The Moviemaker decided to call a break for lunch. And maybe there would even be time for a short nap before going to the mosque for the next shoot.

That night Aabir thought back on the day with a sense of wonderment and a growing sense of pride. He was nobody's fool and had come to an approximate appreciation of the potential of the day's events. He had always known that his qualification as a pilot would attract attention and he had not been disappointed. From the time they had landed in Turkey he had been aware that he had been treated differently and he liked it. Aabir had always craved attention and liked to take centre stage, that's the way he had always been. What he wanted he had always managed to get whether by a smile or a sulk, like when he wanted to be a pilot and his father had balked at the cost, he had simply enlisted the help of his brothers-in-law and the money had come through. He had a fair idea where things were heading and for the moment he was okay with it, eager even. Back home he was just Abbu, one of the guys but here.... Aabir was still smiling when he fell asleep exhausted by the long day.

A few hours away the Moviemaker was having another late night at work. He had just finished editing and splicing the days' shoots and was about to begin uploading them to the numerous cloud databases that he subscribed to. It was tedious but necessary and the Moviemaker believed that what appeared to be excessive caution on the surface would yield unimagined benefits one day. He had a system of cataloguing the shoots according to subject, with subheads for individual details of participants and their role. All role players were catalogued according to name and country of origin and this was cross-referenced with the nature and name of the shoot they had participated in. It had been tough to come up with the system but the long hours had paid off, and the Moviemaker was proud of the end result. What he was creating was multiple indelible cyber tomes of the Islamic State archives which Insha'Allah one day would be available to every Muslim. Every step, every campaign, every sacrifice, would be preserved for eternity, because what went online stayed there forever. He had teams at multiple locations that shifted the data at random intervals to avoid detection and maintain security; he controlled the actions of these teams through a set of protocols and compartmentalization which precluded any one individual, including himself, from tampering with the archives.

The Moviemaker accessed the next cloud server and entered the password. A few seconds later he was at the index and uploading the boy's shoot first. It ran for precisely 3 minutes and 46 seconds. The boy had impressed him on many levels, sure he had been excited by the entire proceeding, but then, he thought, almost everyone enjoyed the novelty of a film shoot the first time. What had impressed him was the patience, it was difficult to sit around doing nothing for several hours, and yes it was doubly difficult to be coached at short notice to deliver a monologue on camera and then deliver a flawless movie clip at the first take, which took some doing and confidence. This one was special; the Moviemaker looked down at the details sheet to enter the name and country of origin. As his fingers drummed a tune over the keyboard he smiled with satisfaction at a task well done.

CHAPTER EIGHT

United States, The East Coast

The call from the One World Group came in the evening when the Contact was out walking the dog. It was very windy and he had to duck behind a clump of trees for better reception over the gale force. He could now hear the caller's voice clearly.

'Good evening, This is Jeremy Tanner, I am operations director at One World Firstly, let me thank you for reaching out to us. We appreciate your confidence. Currently, while we are engaged in research and surveys with regard to Turkey, we do not have any active outreach programme in the area you spoke of.'

The Contact wasn't about to give up yet. 'Are you in any position to help me, or suggest whom I should turn to?' he asked. He had expected the initial company spiel.

The voice stayed official, polite but distant. 'We have examined and considered the contents of your email and while we thank you again for reposing your confidence in us. the specificity of the information that you provided to us neccesitated that we bring it to the notice of the appropriate authority since it would be remiss on our part to inadvertently fail to inform them whenever we come across any information that may have an impact on our national security given the present times.'

The Contact waited patiently for the speaker to finish and arrive at the inevitable logical conclusion to the discussion. When the voice came back, it said, 'We are certainly not averse to working with you on any matter of mutual interest in the future should such a situation arise, but in this instance we have decided to step back due to the obvious intricacies involved. I am sure the authorities which are better placed to address those issues will be contacting you shortly.'

'I understand,' the Contact replied, a grin creasing his features. The dog stood looking up at him clearly impatient to resume the walk. The Contact bent down to ruffle the fur on the dog's shoulders and the animal arched its back in pleasure.

'However, let me reiterate,' his caller continued, 'that we at One World look forward to an opportunity to work with you in the near future'. Both men exchanged the trite and insincere pleasantries that the corporate community affects and then hung up. As the Contact led his dog onward, he was smiling in satisfaction. The One World Group had reacted exactly in the way he had hoped they would. Now he had his 'legit paper trail'.

Maldives

In Malé, Ahmed Idris was sitting in the Dolphin View cafe. From where he sat he could see the international airport. Idris came here regularly. The manager was a friend and the food was delicious, especially the grilled squid.

Idris was deep in thought, and the spectacular view of the ocean his table afforded was lost on him. He had just returned from Zahi's house. He had gone in there and taken the photographs that the Contact wanted. The neighbours had come out their houses and stood silently watching him. They had not asked the usual questions islanders asked visitors: How was the water? What news of the big city? And when he had left he could feel their eyes on his retreating back. The island policeman had stood on the jetty staring at him as the launch edged away from the shore. But that had not upset Idris. It was something else altogether.

His mind went back to the conversation last night, with his wife. She had told him that the Ibraheem women had been seen to become increasingly familiar with two strangers—women—in the children's park. 'Which women?' he had asked immediately. 'Who are they? What are their names?' It seemed that the Ibraheem women had spent a substantial amount of time chatting with these two hijab-clad women for the last couple of months, and about three weeks prior to their departure for Syria, they had started wearing the full hijab themselves. Apparently, nobody knew the identity of these women and now nobody wanted to guess. His wife insisted she didn't know any more than that and he believed her for a reason he couldn't yet fathom. Women had their own grapevine, he knew, and oftentimes it was more accurate than his own. Women on an instinctual level were far more perceptive than men. Idris believed and depended on his wife in more ways than one, but his mind was yet to come to terms with the possibility that there were women in the Maldives who were actively indoctrinating and recruiting on behalf of the Islamic State. For Idris, like for many married men, women's powder room gossip used to be a source of amusement and occasional irritation. Social media chat applications had served the Maldives' female population well. Today, thanks to the Internet, a text message and its response within moments was a far cry from a few years ago when a mother or sister or daughter would go for months before seeing and talking with her kin. A cautious man by nature, Idris had to admit that there was more than a little substance in the rumours about the two veiled women in the public park. He made a mental note to mention it to his friend.

Idris's mind flashed back to his brief exchange of messages with Zahi last night. He had used his new number and had to force himself to be firm, even a bit curt, after she launched a veritable battery of texts that were at times demanding, while others had a beseeching note to them. Their tone clearly indicated that she was on the verge of losing all vestiges of self-control. Last night's exchange had stretched to fifteen minutes, which was far in excess of the Contact's instructions. In the end Idris had hammered home the instructions in no uncertain manner and Zahi had acquiesced to the time limit. Idris remembered the last message sent by Zahi: 'Please get me out of here, brother. I don't want to die here. Please, please, please.' That particular text had kept echoing in his head throughout the day. Perhaps, when there was absolute safety, they could even have a voice call, he mused. He would have to discuss that with the Contact.

This night Idris would instruct her about taking photographs of the areas surrounding her present residence. He reminded himself to tell her to be extremely careful. The only upside of last night's discussion was that he had managed to put recharge her SIM card through a friend in Mumbai and he learnt she had a charger for the phone. That was one less thing to worry about. He took the other phone from its leather pouch, the one with the new number, and scrolled back to the thread of texts from the night before....

> *11.02 Idris:* Zahi. Ahmed here. This is my number. From now on use this only. Not my usual number. I have recharged your SIM so you have credit. Do you have a charger for your cell phone? I need to tell you a few things. Reply when it's safe.
>
> *11.05 Zahi:* Yes I have a charger, Brother get me out of here please, these people lied to me, all of them. I don't want to be here, please tell the police that, tell your friend, that police guy.
>
> *11.07 Idris:* Zahi calm down I need to explain a few things to you. I cannot go to the police. I have contacted a friend who will help us. In the

meanwhile I want you to only read my texts, don't reply immediately. I don't want us texting more than 3 minutes. We can always chat again tomorrow. It's too dangerous for you.

11.08 Zahi: Why can't you go to the police? It's not my fault. These people fooled me. The police and your minister friend will get me released. How is mother? Is she there with you right now? I am in the bathroom so it's safe for me.

11.09 Zahi: The government can send an application and you can come and get me. This place is horrible, yesterday I saw a man getting beaten up and then they shot him. It was horrible, like a mob thing. I can't even go out anywhere without Munsiu or one of the official women. Horrible.

11.12 Idris: Zahi, just shut up and stop texting. I need you to stop texting and stop behaving like a child. The police and government won't help because the whole political system is changed here, it's too complicated to explain over chat. You will learn about it in due course. My friend is arranging for your rescue, I will keep you informed and we will chat everyday if possible but never more than 3 minutes, ok? And I don't want you calling mother or any of your friends or anyone else except me. No email, nothing. If you want to stay alive you have to obey everything I say, understand?

11.13 Zahi: Why only 3 minutes? You mean I am going to die here? No, I don't want to be here, please. And why can't I tell mother? She won't tell anyone, she is our mother. I will give her a short call.

11.15 Idris: You will not call anyone or I will not be able to help you. You understand? As it is we have chatted too long already. Stop behaving like a spoilt brat Zahi. Now switch off your phone and think over what I have said with a calm mind. My friend will help us. I have confidence in him but we must have complete secrecy otherwise you will be in danger. I will text you tomorrow night same time. Be careful with the phone and delete all messages. Keep your phone switched off and hidden.

11.16 Zahi: Ok brother. Please get me out of here, brother. I don't want to die here. Please, please, please.'

The cell phone with the new number went back in the pouch and Idris continued sitting under the awning at Dolphin View. The tall glass of iced tea stood on the table starting to dribble condensation; He occasionally sipped from it and kept staring out at the water, trying not to think, and failing. He glanced at his watch. Time to go home, he thought, but decided to stay for a few minutes more, perhaps even have another iced tea. So Ahmed Idris sat there as dusk approached, and the shadows lengthened along the Malé coastline.

Aleppo, Syria

Zahi couldn't be still for more an a few minutes at a time, and it frightened her. She knew she wasn't her normal self and was scared that her husband or her sisters-in-law would notice. She had visited the bathroom several times and reread all the texts from Ahmed. She knew that she should delete the texts but she couldn't bring herself to do it, and there was so much she didn't understand. Zahi knew herself, she knew that she was somewhat excitable and tended to overreact at times but after initial outbursts she tended to calm down and take things objectively. Although, Allah knew, an overreaction under the given circumstances was perfectly justified.

As she prepared for the afternoon prayer, the Asr, she was alone in the room. Her husband had been out since morning, things had been still strained between them and there had not been much conversation. She couldn't bring herself to chat with her sisters-in-law or brother-in-law. There was a discernable severance of normality. For Zahi the lies and betrayal had resulted in the end of innocence. Well, she thought, as she spread the prayer mat, the honeymoon was definitely over. Zahi went over to the wash basin to perform her wazu before commencing her salah.

Fifteen minutes later, Zahi stood at the window looking out; the pedestal fan whirred behind her and its draft played on her neck and hair, a calmness enveloping her. Perhaps it was the act of prayer, the confidence of faith, or maybe her mind had had time to absorb the shock of her predicament, and the initial panic had subsided, or perhaps it was the calm that only fatalism can bring. She was an intelligent young woman, a graduate of one of the better colleges of Singapore with a degree in marketing, and intended to be a teacher. She went over the texts from her brother in her mind one more time.

The most important item, she realized, was the cell phone. That alone was her lifeline, so where should she keep it? There was not only the instrument but also the charger, although the charger could be kept inconspicuously as an extra without attracting too much attention. And even if she lost it, the Nokia pin charger unit was a pretty generic item and she was sure she would get one even in this place. The suitcase wasn't the answer as a hiding place; it was a shared one, and her handbag out of question. Munsui thought nothing of opening her bag for cash, a pen, and regularly kept his wallet or cell phone there. Anyway, in the event of a search, it would be found within seconds and that was it… finished. Keeping it on her person was an option but the only logical place was her panties, the chances of the instrument slipping through and sliding down her leg were minimal, even then it would be held by the bunched ankle elastic straps of her pajamas. It would be uncomfortable and would require constant adjustments and there would be added complications when she menstruated, but it could be done. Zahi was a practical young woman and she knew rescue was not around the corner, it would take weeks, perhaps several months, if ever. Zahi closed her eyes for a moment. No, she resolved, no negative thinking from now on. She looked around the room for potential hiding places but the room was singularly bare and from what she understood they were liable to be moved to another place any time.

The bathroom, then? Zahi walked to the bathroom door and opened it. The cistern could be ruled out, but her eyes examined the ceiling. Nothing there either, there was no hiding place at all for it. She stepped back, shut the door and walked back to the window. The date palms rustled in a gust of wind and she thought of burying the instrument at its base, rejecting the notion almost immediately. She went across to the cupboard built into the wall, opened it and looked in. It was a recess in the wall about 18 inches deep. Seven horizontal planks of wood, three feet long, served as shelves, Zahi's eyes examined the interior and its contents and for the first time in a week. She smiled. She had found her alternative hiding place: at the bottom of the cupboard lay a large plastic bag of sanitary napkins. Munsiu pretended they didn't exist, far less handle them in any way. So that was part of the problem solved. Zahi intended buying another cell phone when it was permitted—just in case. The regularized citizens had cell phones and she had even seen shops selling electronic goods. Anything was possible. She would be using the cell phone very sparingly, going by what Ahmed had said, so charging the instrument was a minor issue.

She thought about her brother, Ahmed, always the ambitious one and the successful scion of their family. Zahi knew that she had always been his favourite. Ahmed never returned from a trip abroad without bringing something for her. Since she was a baby, he had always been there for her, always supportive, and had never ever failed to respond whenever she wanted anything. Zahi teared up and blinked several times while composing herself. Who was the friend, she wondered, that Ahmed places such faith in? She's never heard Ahmed speak of him before. Whoever it was, may Allah grant him fortitude, and may He grant me the strength to resist calling my mother and my friends. Her hand went to the waistband of her pajamas, the temptation was almost overwhelming.

Zahi stood at the window looking out for a long time, thoughts tumbling over each other in her mind. Then she turned and entered the bathroom again, this time bolting the door behind her. It took a few seconds to power on her cell and another moment to get a signal; she scrolled to messages and one by one deleted each text from her brother. A short time later, the cell phone was switched off and in the cupboard and Zahi left the room to go to the hostel kitchen with a deliberate purpose to her steps. She didn't know how, and she didn't know when, but she was going to get out of Syria.

CHAPTER NINE

The probationer glanced across the room as she flicked her blonde bangs upwards and backwards. She thought Mark Ross looked cute when he was frowning. Her eyes ran over the man who sat with his typical hunch at his desk, a long-forgotten mug of coffee on it. The probationary agent wondered if she should walk across on some pretext and offer to bring him a fresh brew but almost immediately changed her mind. Apart from the fact that several pay-grades separated them, Mark was also a married man. Besides, she had that whole file of satellite imagery analysis to do, and developing a crush on a senior who also happened to be a married man wasn't going to help her any. The probationer returned her attention to the screen on her desk.

The object of the female agent's recent attentions once had dark black hair; it was heavily streaked with white now and his wife often said that the short, neatly-trimmed beard that went with it gave him a distinguished appearance. Mark Ross who looked like an accountant, was a structural engineer by qualification, and an FBI assistant—special agent in charge at the New York office at One Federal Plaza—by profession. Right now he was puzzled, and when Mark Ross was puzzled he frowned. He stared again at the dual screen and the odd mix that the agency filters had thrown at him.

He had entered the subject's details and the agency softwares had immediately kicked in with a preliminary series of broad sweeps across the Internet. These were gradually narrowed by several precision filters as the software started snagging specific details, which were worked further. Two days earlier, Mark had put in a request to the facial recognition unit, and they had uploaded the subjects available, and then pressed the magic button. The system had started running comparisons with tens of millions of probable matches and had taken the full two days to cough up the few results that it had. The subject had appeared in the oddest of places: on a mountain trail in the Helmund province of Afghanistan, in a single satellite image at the edge of the remote parking bay at Heathrow Airport, and a few others. Except for one photograph, which showed him with a bunch of men in combat gear at a training centre in India, the subject appeared alone, almost as if he shunned human company—or least avoided being photographed with them.

Mark hunched further forward as he brought up another browser. The subject's biometrics had turned up zero. He had obviously never been arrested anywhere before, or if he had, he had not been fingerprinted. The only fingerprint record of the subject in the United States was reflected in the archives of the United States Citizenship and Immigration Services (USCIS), and at the Department of Motor Vehicles. The subject hadn't left the United States in the last two years and displayed every characteristic of a retired man. He had a healthy insurance policy and his house was free of loans. Mark had conducted a cursory examination of the subject's bank and credit history, and nothing had jumped out at him. The man paid his bills on time and had a portfolio of stocks and bond investments that averaged 1,25,000 dollars a year.

Mark had also tapped into the local and international community of Law Enforcement Officers (LEOs) and intelligence agencies, both retired and serving, and the feedback so far perplexed him further. It appeared that some old-timers acknowledged the subject's existence but were curiously reluctant to talk about him. Either that, Mark thought, or they didn't know much. He had touched base with an old MI5 acquaintance of his that morning, and the normally precise Englishman had been momentarily silent after hearing the name, and then grunted,

'Him? That's some piece of work there, mate. Fucking technician, that one,' and then rung off.

So Mark sat there and continued trying to put together a profile of the man who had such precise information about a family of Maldivians, that had left their homeland in response to a call from the Islamic State, to wage Jihad in what was conceivably the most godforsaken part of the world today. His partner Chris had already been in touch with the field office in Turkey, and the file was building up steadily. The biggest concern was the young man, Aabir, who had come to the United States and had obtained his pilot's licence. That part had checked out, as had every other detail so far. The local FBI unit had interviewed the flight instructor, and by all accounts, Aabir was a smart, friendly young man. The instructor had apparently no reason to suspect anything and, indeed, according to the agent who had interviewed him, had seemed very much taken aback by the line of questioning. He had even given Aabir's email address and Maldives phone number. Aabir had kept in touch with his instructor as recently as six weeks ago. They already had the number he used when he was in the United States and the call details had been analyzed. Nothing suspicious there. Aabir had been a rich, carefree young man, as long as he had been in the United States. What could have happened after that? In the last six weeks? Mark wondered how an entire family got radicalized in less than two months. How, in the name of god, does that happen?

A thought struck him, and he looked into licences. A couple of minutes later it turned out that the subject had neither applied for, nor had been granted a licence to possess a firearm anywhere in the United States. Nor was he a member of any registered club or social organization.

A couple of hours later, Mark finished what he had on the file, was mildly irritated at how little he had been able to uncover, despite the resources at his command—irritated and more than a little intrigued. There was that thing on the Balochistan border which was definitely linked with the subject, but it had been brief and very violent and dirty, and not many details were available, and the overall picture remained unclear. Ross had hit a brick wall when he made a couple of calls to the few parties involved that he could trace. He had done the most he could at that stage and would have to set up a meet with this *extraordinary character* at the earliest. He could sense there was more information coming up and, truth be told, he was looking forward to the face-to-face. He picked up the phone and dialled the number, his pencil tapping a steady beat on the subject's file.

The Contact was grinding his teeth in his sleep when the call came. The dog's ears pricked up uneasily as the Contact's body moved restlessly on the sheets and the sweat slowly darkened the pillow covers. The dog whined softly, and it was that, more than the phone, that woke the Contact up. He woke up slowly and in stages, aware of a dream which he couldn't remember but still sense and of a dull ache over his eyes. He had had one of his bad dreams, he realized, and turned his head to his right. The bottle of water was there, and he picked it up and guzzled its contents in one long greedy draught, stopping only when it was empty. He sat up stiffly, swinging his legs over the side. As usual his limbs and head ached after he dreamed, as if his body had contracted itself painfully. He instinctively reached out to stroke the dog's head, feeling again the curious sense of loss and emptiness.

The Contact shrugged off the feelings of nothingness; he was long accustomed to them. The devil was never in the details, but rather the devil lurked in the shadows of nightmares he reminisced fleetingly. He picked up the phone, The number was not known to him.

'Hello.'

'Hi, good afternoon, this is assistant special agent-in-charge Mark Ross of the FBI. I hope I haven't called you at an inconvenient time.' The voice was low, almost conversational, and the Contact smiled in admiration of the technique. The perfect modulation invited confidences and dialogue.This was no greenfoot.

'Hello, Mark, I was about to give up on you guys. What took you so long?' The Contact kept his tone convivial, just two friends chatting, end of a hard day, time to start on a six-pack sort of thing.

'Oh, I've been pretty busy these days, you know how it is,' responded Mark. 'You recently got in touch with the One World Group, I'm told, and we would like to meet you about the obviously detailed information you possess.'

'Yeah, sure,' the Contact said. 'Where do you suggest?'

'Well, sir, do you come down to New York City ever? We could meet up somewhere downtown or alternatively, my partner and I would be glad to drive across to your neck of the woods.'

'NYC is fine with me,' the Contact said. 'I like to walk in the city in this season.'

'Oh, that's great, then, shall we say tomorrow? I can manage between 11.00 to 2.30 anytime, so pick whatever is convenient for you. We can do it the day after too, but it would have to be in the evening.'

'Tomorrow works for me,' the Contact replied. 'Let's meet at 12.30, maybe grab a sandwich somewhere.'

'Fantastic, we could meet up at Terry's if that's okay with you, they make a great sandwich,' Mark said. 'I'll text you the address from my cell phone. That way, you'll have my number too.'

The Contact put down his phone and nodded to himself in satisfaction. He replayed the conversation in his mind. ASAC Mark Ross had been professional and pretty much textbook in his approach. He had done a fairly good job of establishing a workable rapport within a two-minute phone conversation that included a greeting, small talk and an appointment all rolled into one. Not bad, the Contact thought, not bad at all, as he walked to the bathroom for a quick shower before taking the dog out. The alert animal was already watching him in anticipation, its head resting on its forepaws.

That night, the Contact's first call was from Idris, in the Maldives.

'Hello, my friend,' the Contact answered on picking up the phone.

'I just got off from texting Zahi. I passed on the instructions,' Idris said.

'And?' The Contact waited for more.

'Well, it was rough at first, gave me a few anxious moments, but I think she is on board now,' replied Idris. 'Today, we were in contact for exactly two and a half minutes. I asked her to take no risks and that it was all right to miss a few days if required.' He added his own query. 'What about the pictures you asked me to take of her house? What do want me to do with them?'

'Hang on to them,' the Contact replied. 'Send me copies and I will tell you when we need them and what to do.'

'Any progress from your side?' The plea in Idris's voice was unmistakeable.

'Yes, my friend. I will be meeting some authorities tomorrow so we shall talk further then. For now, you should know that I am hoping for some official help.'

'That's good to hear.' Idris leaned back in his chair and twisted his head and shoulders left to right, to ease his tense neck muscles. Right, I'll speak to you tomorrow, then.'

The second caller was the softspoken Doctor Sameer Ibraheem.

'Hi, this is Sameer.'

'Hello, Sameer, what is the latest? Are you still being followed?'

'I have avoided going out,' replied the doctor. 'Just staying with my parents for the time being—as you suggested. Most things can be accomplished over the phone anyway.' The doctor went on to add, 'But I would have to get back home to my wife in a day or two at the most.'

The Contact responded with another question. 'Were you able to have a chat with any of their friends or social media groups?'

'I'm *trying*,' the doctor couldn't mask the fustration in his voice. 'I did call up several friends of theirs but nobody seems to know anything.' His voice trailed off and for a while both men were silent.

The Contact spoke first. 'Very well, tomorrow I may meet some people who are experienced at this sort of thing, so let's hope I can get their cooperation.'

'Yes, Inshallah, your friends can help me and my parents. I hope so,' the doctor's voice broke now, 'for my parents' sake... this is all very difficult....'

'I understand, I do,' said the Contact. 'Call me tomorrow, all right?'

Both men hung up. The Contact went into his kitchen and opened the cabinet where he kept his liquor. Puring himself a single malt, he walked out onto the deck, and looked down into the pond. There was enough moonlight for him to make out the pale forms of the koi as they swam near the surface of the water, darting into and from under the artificial waterfall. He did not want to get closer to the pond's edge for fear of spooking them; they would then all dive down to the bottom and stay there till he left. The Contact stood there for a long time, the glass in his hand resting on the railings. He took the occasional sip as he peered down into the pond, still immersed in his own thoughts. Sometime later, he came inside and glanced at the digital clock on the desk. It was mid-morning in India. He reached for his cell phone and searched his list till he found the name he was looking for. Settling himself in his chair, he dialled.

It was 10.15 am in Mumbai, and Raoul Miranda was sitting in his office in Lower Parel. He sweated constantly, despite the air conditioner running on full blast just feet away from him, and had taken to draping a napkin around his thick neck, the edges of which were visible under the collar of his shirt. Raoul was a big bull of a man with legs like tree-trunks but he moved surprisingly quickly and nimbly for a man of his size, and was the object of murmurs of appreciation on the dance floor whenever the mood over took him, which was often. A travel agent by occupation, he had also a quiet, profitable sideline in 'documentation' as he preferred to call it; on the other hand simply used the terms 'forgery' and 'counterfeiting' for the same thing. He had never been arrested, never known to have betrayed a client, and his documents were as good as the real McCoy. The contact had used him several times over the years and Raoul had never failed to deliver. The big man reached over and picked up the handset.

'Avon international travel agency, how may I help you?'

'Hi Raoul, it's me, your friend from the Big Apple,' said the Contact. In Mumbai, Raoul Miranda's face creased into a smile. He genuinely liked the Contact and besides, the man always made prompt and full payments without haggling.

'Hello, old friend, what can I do for you today?' he asked.

'A simple job this time, amigo, please. I want a complete set of bona fides for an Indian, female. There is no chance of a stand-in for the interview so I am afraid it will have to be non-biometric. Charge me for that too, and there will be some stamping required for the report card.'

Raoul knew exactly what the Contact meant. 'Not a problem, my friend. I assume there is a rush on this?' he queried.

'I would appreciate if it could be hastened, yes,' the Contact replied. 'I will send you the pictures and details through the drop box as usual then, along with the advance?' He paused before advancing the knowledge of his travel plans. 'I should be there in a few weeks to collect; I assume it will be the usual set?'

'Yes, a full set, so send me different photos. If that's a problem, don't sweat it. I can Photoshop,' Raoul replied. Both men rang off.

The Contact sat for a few more minutes. He wrote and sent an email using a little-used id. He would check for a reply sometime tomorrow. Before going to the bedroom he rinsed and placed the glass on the kitchen counter. Tomorrow would be a long day.

Mark Ross and his partner Chris Bellamy had a problem on their hands, two problems to be precise. The first was that they found themselves hopelessly unable to control the meeting and to direct, indeed dominate, the conversational flow. The second problem was more personal: it was hard not to stare at this man and harder still not to feel distinctly somehow... well, *small*. The last time Mark had felt this way was back at Quantico on his first day of training when an old-timer had accosted him in the corridors and with a few incisive questions had effectively and quickly plumbed the depths of his ignorance.

They had parked a couple of blocks away and had walked into Terry's about a quarter of an hour before schedule. As usual, there was a lot of customer traffic, predominantly students, and the place's proximity to the park was an added attraction. It was one of the reasons they had chosen Terry's, figuring that it would make the subject feel more secure. It was standard operating procedure for first-time meets.

The first surprise came when the man waved at them as soon as they entered. That wasn't how it was supposed to work. They knew his face, but he didn't know theirs. They had no option but to walk over to the corner table where the subject sat. Mark spoke first. 'Hi, I'm Mark Ross, we spoke yesterday on the phone.'

The subject had nodded and the two men shook hands. Mark introduced Chris and they decided to order takeout sandwiches and coffees and sit on one of the benches in the park. The sandwiches arrived quickly and the man insisted on paying for them. He was wearing jeans and a flannel shirt with a corduroy jacket, and when he stood up, he loomed over Ross, who was no midget at 5'11. It was their 'subject' who led them out of the door with the two agents following—'like bloody schoolboys', Mark Ross thought bemusedly, as he glanced across at his partner who met his look with an upward flick of his right eyebrow. They found a bench away from the others and settled down. A rather bold and obviously experienced squirrel approached their table, squatting with its forepaws in the air, facing them a few feet away, clear confident of some delectable crusts coming his way in good time.

'We found the email you sent to the One World Group very interesting,' Mark began. 'Naturally, its contents are of concern to us, particularly when viewed in context of the threat from terrorism and any impact it may have on national security…'

'Yes, I have some more details on the family and more on the way,' the Contact interjected, and reached into his shirt pocket. He produced two folded pages of printed notes, which he handed over to the agent.

Mark Ross poured over the notes. They were clear and succinct, omitting no detail and, in essence, answering every question that he had formulated for the meeting. He looked up and said, 'These are very precise, like a professional report.'

'Yes, I thought it would help you,' the Contact smiled, ignoring the ring of condescension. It was an astonishingly charming smile that made both men beam instinctively back. The Contact looked steadily at the men sitting across him.

'As I said, we have access to more information. I know that the family has reached Syria.'

'They have?' Mark Ross was unable to disguise the surprise in his voice. 'How do we know that?'

'One of the family, a newly married daughter-in-law, managed to sent a text through to her brother. She was deceived into accompanying her husband on his journey. She is smart and educated and the others do not know about her establishing secret communications with anyone else.' The Contact continued, his eyes locked into Mark's, 'She is an asset, and you agree that can be useful. I am not asking for the impossible here, just help me get her out.' He paused before adding on a note of plea, 'The others are there because they want to be, not her.' He stopped speaking.

The agents leaned back, digesting the information. Mark's brain was on temporary overdrive with the implications and the possibilities it involved. There was no doubt about what the Contact was offering: *Milk the cow but then get her out, there was to be no sacrifice at the altar of collateral damage*. They were acutely aware that the US-trained and -qualified pilot was a hugely significant threat, but to have an uncontaminated asset in Raqqa itself! This could be big. It was cases such as these that make or break careers.

The FBI man looked across at the Contact and nodded. 'I will need to get back to you on this, of course.'

'Of course,' echoed the Contact, 'I just want to add that there are many Maldivian nationals in the theatre, and these guys do call back home, as you know,' he paused. 'Now I think that the United States has so far not been able to appraise the exact dimensions of threat the Maldives poses in so far as the Islamic State goes, and the resultant fallout when it comes to security in South-East Asia, China and security's increasing role in the Maldives in particular.'

Mark and Chris looked at each other. Both men knew that China had been actively building up a relationship with the Maldives on a level affecting global security and the balance of power including the commercial. The intention was obvious. But was there something they didn't know? For a country with the resources it had, the Maldives was a definite 'nothing' in significance, except, perhaps geo-strategically. 'Was this the sweetener?' Mark Ross wondered. 'Or was the man bringing something more to the table?' He watched the Contact as the man took another bite of his sandwich. He had ordered tuna on wheat with avocado and black olives, and was obviously enjoying it. The squirrel had come closer, just a couple of feet from the Contact who tossed it a small bit. The squirrel actually grabbed it in mid-air, and all three of them laughed.

The Contact reached into his jacket pocket this time, producing a noticeably thicker sheaf of papers and slid it across the table. He kept his hand on it as he spoke: 'This is my approximation of the state of affairs in the Maldives today, you may find it of some value. Naturally, I can amplify on specific points if needed.' The Contact made a slow languid motion with his hand, his palm facing up.

Mark Ross hefted the papers; there had to be at least twenty pages there, he estimated. A cursory look at the first page told him that it was drafted in the same crisp manner, precise and rich in detail. The analysts back at the office would swoon in delight, he thought as he tucked the papers away. There was nothing else to discuss, he realized, certainly nothing right now, without reporting back to the office and sorting through the details.

'Well, I will get back to you on this. It may take a couple of days,' said Mark, getting up. His partner followed suit.

'You could have your boys ask around the jewellery stores in Gaziantep. They are unlikely to take all that gold into Syria,' the Contact said.

Mark nodded slowly, the possibility hadn't occurred to him. Maybe they had converted the jewellery into cash and who knew what that thread might unravel? 'Anything else?' he asked.

'Not right now,' the Contact replied and watched the two agents walking back to their car. He tossed another crust towards the squirrel and then turned his full attention to his sandwich.

Mark Ross and Chris Bellamy reached their car and got inside. They looked at each other without expression

'Well, I'll be goddamned!' said Chris.

Chapter TEN

Malé

The small purple crafts were the hardest to hit, they seemed to jump outwards and away from the red tracers almost every time resulting in a miss. The youngster instinctively recognized this and compensated with a shift in strategy, his fingers lightning-fast over the console and on the toggle. Ahmed Idris watched his son bounce the tracers off the sidewalls and no less than three purple crafts burst apart and swirled crazily downwards. Idris had tried the video game a few times and found he was woefully short on the dexterity and hand-eye coordination required even at the beginners' level. Youngsters today seem born with these skills, he thought, although he wished his son would take more interest in outdoor activities. Why, for instance, could the boy not swim? That was unthinkable for an islander.

Idris turned back to look at his guest, his friend Salim of the Maldives Police Sensitive and Confidential Unit. Salim had demurred at visiting Idris's office or meeting him in any place public in Malé. Arranging and coordinating a meet on some island on another atoll was both inconvenient and time-consuming. So Salim had elected to visit his apartment in Malé. There were many other houses in the apartment block and therefore it was sufficiently discreet.

The Contact had asked Idris to make enquiries into the radicalism and recruitment scene in the Maldives and the businessman had made a few careful choices, Salim amongst them, to approach for information. What the Contact wanted was a brief on the organizations and people engaged in recruitment and radicalization and the source of funding, names, phone numbers and the like. Idris didn't know why the Contact wanted these details but he knew that it was important and that was all the reason he required. Salim would help as much as he could although there had been a few bad moments when it came to his asking who wanted the information. Idris's explanation, that he was personally curious, especially because of Zahi's departure, sounded lame and even as he spoke he could see the disbelief and worse, the alarm in Salim's eyes. Idris had immediately back-pedalled, revised tactics and had come up with a watered-down version of the truth—he had engaged a 'specialist' in these things—and was hoping for the best, but the inevitable questions had followed.

'Who is this guy? How did you come to know of him?' Salim had asked.

'He is from the UK, we have a common friend, someone who was with me at University,' Idris had replied.

'And he is what? Ex-SAS? Special Forces?' the policeman had asked, leaning forward, his eyes locked with Idris's and unblinking.

'Something like that, Salim, I, er, really don't know much, actually, it was an impulsive sort of thing, I mean I don't know what's going to come of it.'

'Well, he must be costly, these Brits charge you an arm and a leg,' observed Salim and asked again, 'How do you communicate with him then? Phone? Email?'

'Er,' Idris's brain raced to cope with the unexpected turn the conversation had taken, 'he did call me a couple of times and we are in communication through email as well, You know how much I am worried about Zahi.'

'Yes, yes, my friend, I am simply curious about this guy. I mean, I hope he is reliable and not just out to make a quick buck,' Salim said, and left soon thereafter. Ahmed Idris noticed that Salim pressed the elevator button to go down only after it had reached the top floor and had disgorged its occupants. No doubt he had made sure to board an empty elevator on his way up too.

As Idris watched his friend Salim cross the road to his car from his balcony, he was acutely aware that he had been measured and somehow found wanting.

New York City, United States

In One Federal Plaza Mark Ross was examining the country profile on the Maldives, the frown in place again. Chris had to take off to follow up on an ongoing investigation and they would meet up in the evening around 5 to compare notes. In the meantime, it was agreed that Mark would bone up on the Maldives while Chris would talk to the analysts about the brief that the Contact had so nonchalantly sprung on them. The conversation on the way back from the meeting had been typically Chris.

'Well, I will be goddamned,' Chris had said, his eyes flicking over the sidewalk.

'Oh yes,' Mark had said, 'that was a bit out of left field'.

'Out of left field?' his partner had swung around in the agency car, eyes popping, 'out…?!' Chris spluttered, 'Bro, we got out-manoeuvered, out-strategized, and let's be frank here, out everything!'

Mark had looked across at his partner and nodded ruefully, 'Yep, we looked like a couple of freshmen out there.'

Mark adjusted the spectacles higher up on his nose as he recollected his partner's and disbelief. Well, he thought, we will exchange notes later... for now he had the agency's' country brief in front of him. He had just called out for a coffee barely ten minutes ago and already it stood forgotten inches away from his left elbow. Mark stretched out his legs and settled down to read the 10-page document.

Buddhism had been the dominant religion in the Maldives and enjoyed royal patronage for well over thousand five hundred years. Almost all archaeological remains in the Maldives are Buddhist in origin, these mainly consisting of stupas and monasteries, and all artifacts found to date bear typical Buddhist iconography. Since building space and materials had always been scarce in that tiny land, the Maldivians usually constructed their places of worship on the foundations of previous monuments. The Maldivian language, the initial script, the architecture, ruling and governance institutions, customs and traditions had evolved when the Maldives was a Buddhist kingdom.

Adhering to a typically Islamic concept, that before Islam there was a period of jahiliyya, or ignorance. The history books used by the Maldivian educational system tout the introduction of Islam at the end of the 12th century to be considered as the cornerstone of the country's history.

The Middle East primarily became interested in Maldives due to its strategic location and its abundant supply of cowrie shells. The shells were a form of currency that was widely used throughout Asia and along the East African coastline since ancient times. Middle-Eastern seafarers had just begun to exert dominion over the Indian Ocean trade routes in the 10th century, and Maldives was an important link in those routes.

The importance and consequential dependence on the Arabs in their role as traders in the Indian Ocean is a vital factor that influenced the conversion of the last Buddhist king of the Maldives to Islam somewhere in the latter half of the 11th century. This ushered in the era of the sultans. Muhammad al Adil, as the first sultan chose to be called, initiated a series of six Islamic dynasties consisting of 84 sultans that lasted until

1932, when the sultanate became elective. Thus, the Maldives was perhaps the last region in south Asia to be totally converted to Islam.

Mark reached for the coffee while reading and absentmindedly took a sip, his cheeks creasing into a grimace almost immediately. He briefly considered walking across the office to the pantry and using the microwave to reheat the brew, but decided it wasn't worth the effort, the coffee would more likely taste worse. He slid open a drawer, searched for and found a packet of gum, slid out a couple of strips, popped them into his mouth and returned his attention to the brief.

The Maldives had gained independence in 1965, which effectively ended its 'dependency relationship' with Britain. This however did not realign or in any way alter the 'power equation' when it came to its social structure or distribution of wealth, as it did in other countries that the Crown had ruled. The Brits, moreover, managed to wrangle a deal which allowed them the use of two strategically placed islands, Gan and Hitaddu, the first to be used as an airfield and the second to house radio masts and installations.

These islands had an interesting history. In 1959, a local secessionist movement in the southern atolls, that benefited economically from the British presence on Gan, severed ties with the Maldives government and formed an independent state with Abdulla Afeef Didi as president. This British-engineered coup resulted in a new country called the United Suvadivan Republic, had a combined population of around 30,000 loosely scattered in the atolls that are now called North Huvadu and South Huvadu, including parts of atolls Addu and Fua Mulaku. The United Suvadian Republic died in its infancy, surviving less than four years, from 1959 to 1962. In '62 President Nasir sent gunboats from Malé to eliminate elements opposed to his rule. Abdulla Afeef Didi fled to the then British colony of Seychelles, where, naturally he was granted political asylum.

The usual suspects continued to hold sway over the old structures of complete domination and the same elite continued to rule society and dictate polity. From 1978 to 2008, Maldives was ruled by President Gayoom. He had absolute power over the executive and the judiciary. Political persecution, imprisonment and killings were his other tools of governance. Come 2004, there was mounting pressure for reforms and multiparty elections led President Gayoom to embark on democratic reforms which assisted in recognizing political parties and adopting a new constitution that guaranteed judicial and police reforms, freedom of expression, assembly and establishment of the human rights commission. This also included gender parity for constitutional posts, as well as the presidency.

In Maldives, the first democratic elections were held in 2008 and the first multi-party parliamentary elections were held in May 2009. In August 2008, the new constitution was adopted, bringing an end to the authoritarian regime, which had been in place since 1965. The new Constitution paved the way for devolution of powers, which were concentrated previously in the hands of the president. The Maldivian Democratic Party (MDP) came to power with a promise of institutionalizing democratic institutions and protecting human rights in the country. After three decades of authoritarian rule that ended in 2008, and despite its internal political and economic problems, the foreign policy of Maldives was finally aimed at maintaining friendly relations with other countries. Mohamed Nasheed became president.

The transition of Maldives from an authoritarian state to a democratic one was appreciated by the international community. However, this transition presented a number of challenges in terms of strengthening democratic institutions and structures, such as the judiciary, and promoting freedom of expression as well as rule of law.

However, political developments in the country followed a ragged trajectory. Even though it had adopted a new Constitution, the zero cohesion between political parties on issues like judicial independence, presidential powers and parliamentary functions created an atmosphere of distrust and uncertainty regarding policy and its implementation thereof. The political system, with a directly elected president and parliament (majlis) created opportunities for several players to contest elections and form alliances, usually with business leaders and commercial groups, to prop up their interests. The resulting dogfight led to the creation of the Progressive Party of Maldives (PPM), under the leadership of Gayoom.

These arrangements only increased political tensions between the president and the majlis, ultimately culminating in the resignation of Nasheed as president. It was a case of too much too soon. A number of unpopular political, judicial and economic decisions led to the mobilization of opposition against Nasheed. There was the case of the government entering into a contract with the Indian infrastructure company, GMR, without the consent of the majlis. It was a huge contract and the financial implications alone were a matter of interest to other parties.

There were other issues, such as the arrest of opposition parties' leaders, and then, the removal of the chief justice of the criminal court turned out to be the factor that tipped the balance of power. The opposition, with its three decades of a deeply entrenched support system, went into overdrive and claimed that those acts were unconstitutional. In addition, they evoked anti-India sentiments to garner public support against President Nasheed. Nasheed was very friendly with India and the opposition used this as a talking point to discredit his integrity and intentions.

Dr Mohammed Waheed Hassan, the then vice-president, took over office as president in 2012, with the support of all political parties except the MDP, and formed a 'Unity Government'. Following Mohamed Nasheed's allegations that he had been forced to resign in 2012, a commission was established to look into the events leading up to and following the date of the resignation. Nobody was surprised when the report declared that the resignation was legal and that there was 'no illegally coerced resignation of the President on 7 February 2012, and that the subsequent transfer of power followed precisely the prescriptions of the Constitution'.

Initially, Nasheed accepted the report with some reservations, but in January 2013, he asked for a review of the report and the Maldives remained in a political deadlock till the 2013 elections.

A threat to Islam, rising extremism and threat to the sovereignty of the country from external actors became the key election issues and the PPM alleged that Nasheed was an agent of external forces. The elections in 2013 were coloured by various irregularities, allegations and counter-allegations about its legitimacy. Since both the candidates, Nasheed of the MDP and Abdulla Yameen of the PPM, failed to secure the 50 per cent mark in the first round, a second round of elections was conducted in November 2013.

The intervening period helped the PPM leadership to mobilize public opinion against Nasheed and also helped in securing an alliance with the Jumhoori Party (JP). The Jumhoori Party got 23 per cent of the votes in the first round. The alliance helped Abdulla Yameen to take charge as president. It helped that the judiciary was totally pro-Yameen, and had removed the election commissioner, which no doubt helped.

Mohamed Nasheed was arrested and a battery of charges, including that of terrorism, were levelled against him. He still had a sizeable following which resorted to democratic protests and managed to garner the support of the international community in which the United Kingdom naturally played a major part and India chose to minimize its role. The eminent human rights lawyer and wife of the Hollywood star George Clooney, Amal Clooney, took up Nasheed's case, which made it suitably high-profile. On the other side, the newly formed Maldivian government engaged the services of Cherie Blair, the wife of former UK Prime Minister Tony Blair, ostensibly to 'improve the image of the Maldives', which was polispeak for damage control in the international community in terms of public relations. Things came to a head internally and externally, and to ease the pressure, President Yameen chose to 'lance the boil' by granting a release on medical grounds to Nasheed, who flew to the United Kingdom, promptly applied for and received asylum, both the majlis and the business community heaved a collective sigh of relief.

In the last year, the opposition continued to be vocal in its protest against what was evidently a regime rule directed by Maumoon Gayoom by proxy, since the president, Abdulla Yameen, was no other than his half-brother.

Radical Islamization of society, health care, gender parity, freedom of press, corruption and unemployment were the burning issues in the Maldives. There were instances of groups marching in Malé carrying Islamic State flags and calling for the implementation of the Islamic Sharia law, and demolition of Buddhist relics by radical groups. Allegations by the former foreign minister, Ahmed Naseem, that the 'Islamic Ministry of Maldives had a role in sending 200 Maldivians to fight the ISIS war in Syria', were strongly condemned by the Islamic minister, Dr Mohammed Shaheem. The Kingdom of Saudi Arabia entered into an agreement with the Government of Maldives to 'improve and establish the proper Islamic values in the State', thus steering the course of the state towards the shores of Dabiq. For Saudi Arabia, the resources involved were less than negligible, even nonexistent. That kingdom spent more on the hotel tariffs of any one of the extended royal family than in a year on the Maldives. The judiciary was composed primarily of old-timers and sufficiently devolved from the state, so that its diktat was binding on the president. Each recognized the lifeline that the other offered and the majlis completed the trinity of regime rule, religion and reciprocity.

As news of more and more Maldivians leaving to join the ISIS, or in some cases the Jabhat al Nusra, trickled out and caught the attention of the international media, the opposition, egged on by Nasheed, who was safely ensconced in the UK, started agitating and the usual horse-trading commenced. To add to the mix there was a falling-out between Abdulla Yameen and his deputy Ahmed Adeeb over some cash which appeared to have been generated under questionable circumstances and had now gone 'missing'. It was therefore imperative to arrest the deputy, and days later, while the President Yameen was travelling in his launch to the capital, there was an explosion which turned out to be a bomb placed under the presidential seat. Coincidentally, the Yameen was not in his seat and remained unhurt. What was more providential was that the 'bomb' merely wrecked the seat and there was no other damage to the launch, which sailed serenely on to its destination without stop. It was a curiously weak bomb, but it sufficed to form the basis of an 'assassination plot masterminded by the president's deputy' and handcuffs were slapped on Adeeb the moment his plane touched ground at Malé airport.

As the foreign media became more active, a businessmen's corsortium in the Maldives came to the conclusion that the adverse publicity was detrimental to commerce and appealed to the president to impose a blanket ban on all foreign journalists. And to silence the local voices of dissent, the president touted and got the approval, on 9 August 2016 from the country's parliament, for adopting the 'Protection of Reputation and Good Name and Freedom of Expression Bill'. The bill criminalized speech deemed to be defamatory, comment against 'any tenet of Islam', to 'threaten national security' or to 'contradict general social norms'.

The broad grounds for restrictions in the bill contradicted not only international human rights standards recognized by the Maldives, such as the International Covenant on Civil and Political Rights, but also its own constitution, which protects the right to freedom of expression. Criminalizing speech on such vague and broad grounds as set out in the bill was a blatant strategy to muzzle the press and imprison dissenters. Islam was being used as a ground for limiting free speech and peaceful democratic dissent.

Recently, there had been an exposé of money-laundering allegedly done at the behest of the president himself, and with the active participation of the National Bank. This had been telecast via the *Al Jazeera* channel.

All in all, Mark thought, the country was like a keg of dynamite capped by a sputtering fuse of Islamic radicalization. Why, the capital was barely a tenth of the size of a single New York Avenue! And to face such a multitude of issues, a country with a population barely nudging 350,000. Mark shook his head bemusedly. He had done a Google survey of the capital city, Malé, and seriously doubted that any car with a respectable engine output would have enough road length to get into third gear. What a godawful mess of a country! He shook his head again, laid down the brief and glanced at his watch. It was time for the evening meeting for the other thing, and after that, he would link up with Chris. Mark made sure the sheaf of notes the Contact had handed over was in the folder and moved toward the conference rooms. He grinned wryly as he imagined the look on his division chief's face when he had a look at the contents. As he picked up pace, Mark's grin broadened.

Raqqa

Zahi had the feeling that she was being alienated. She had spent the day with her sisters-in-law and the other women and was aware of more than a few slyly exchanged looks when they thought she wasn't looking, and there were those muted conversations that seem to come to an abrupt halt as soon as she approached. It had been going on for the last few days, and it had been only today, when she was talking to Nabeela, that it dawned on her. Nabeela was her age and like her, newly married. Although she was happy to be here in Al Sham and had been here considerably longer, she too seemed to be treated differently. Zahi saw that she was by herself more often than not and that Nabeela seemed more animated when they were together. She also found that Nabeela was a British citizen and had a degree in marketing.

So! It's the fact that I am educated that makes me different to the others, my college degree and my exposure to western culture and behaviour that places a question mark on my values and purpose. And here, it doesn't help that I am beautiful, even if I am married and I wear the hijab. For these people, I am tainted and shall always remain so. Zahi turned on her side and stared at the wall opposite. Soon it would be close to eleven, and she could send and receive a text or maybe two. She already knew what she was going to text:

> 'Dear Brother, I couldn't take any pictures today, we didn't go out at all. They say we will be going to the market the day after. The others don't like me. I know you must be making arrangements to get me out and I am waiting, love Zahi.'

In the United States, the Contact was on the phone with an old acquaintance, Captain Brar.

'So, there is just this one cargo?' Captain Brar had the raspy voice that was the byproduct of a score of cigarettes a day for a score of years. He sat in his cabin on board the *Star of the East*, a dozen nautical miles off the Dubai coastline, and leaned forward to tap out the half-inch of ash on his John Player. Brar was a tall man who had a way of sitting erect in a La-Z-Boy that the Contact had never seen before.

'Yes, I will make sure it clears Customs and Ports and your account will be credited at the time of delivery,' the Contact kept his tone conversational. 'Of course, the usual advance will be transferred the day before.'

'Oh? An express job is it?' The contact could almost hear the smile in the captain's voice and the chuckle that followed confirmed it. Involuntarily, he smiled himself.

'Something like that. Anyway, we've got to work on your berthing schedule and I may have to ask you to delay, but no more than a couple of hours, and there will be extras for that.' The Contact continued, 'I will be in touch about my itinerary. I will, most probably, meet you in a week or so.' Both men rang off.

An hour later, the Contact was standing on his front porch, a smile of pure unadulterated delight on his face. His friend had returned and the parakeets were on their way back home. No more frenetic chirping, no more birdseed, discarded feathers and the smell of birdshit! The dog stood by his side, its tail wagging.

CHAPTER ELEVEN

The taxi driver nudged the light indicator lever downwards and the Contact swayed as they turned to the right, the tires hissing on the slick rain-swept road. He could now see the shining lights of the Burj Khaleefa directly ahead, alternatively diffusing and brightening as the windshield wipers flicked away. As the taxi glided ahead, the Contact glanced at his watch. Just in time, he thought, for a meal at the Al Hallab restuarant in Quasais, before retiring for the night. Tomorrow was going to be a long day and he hoped to get a lot done before he started on the next leg of his trip.

The Contact had initially intended to visit Dubai after a couple of weeks but two events decreed that he advance his schedule. Firstly, Captain Brar had announced a change in his sailing itinerary and therefore their next meeting would have been delayed by two more weeks, and secondly, another man that the Contact wanted to meet had coincidentally arrived in the UAE. This, coupled with the fact that he really didn't have anything to do over the weekend, made a trip to Dubai a no-brainer. There also was the fact that in the UAE, Sunday was not a holiday and the weekend started on Thursday evenings.

The Contact was quite at home in the city and familiar with its landmarks, yet, during the short taxi ride from the newly constructed Terminal 5 to the Bur Dubai area, where he had made reservations at a service apartment, he noted yet another flyover which hadn't been there on his last visit. The city seemed to be imploding with construction works, despite its small landmass.

The taxi pulled up with another hiss as the brakes compensated for the unseasonal bout of rain, and the Contact handed the driver a 50 dirham note, indicating with an outstretched palm that he should keep the change. The driver murmured his appreciation as the Contact stepped out onto the steaming street and hurried into the lobby of the service apartment. Check-in formalities took a few minutes and an hour later, he was out on the streets again, in another cab, headed towards the Al Hallab, a restaurant which he favoured for its exquisite Lebanese cuisine. He loved the bread and baba ganoush they served, and the kebabs were legendary.

As the taxi curved along the clock tower roundabout, the Contact looked out at the bright lights and wondered at how much strategic marketing and a providential geography could contribute towards making a small strip of sand with no oil deposits, barely the size of a small county back in the US, a booming commercial hub with some of the most expensive real estate in the world. The reasons, he thought, must lie in the concentration of wealth with the royals, a competitive expatriate population and a specially tuned banking and economic system which allowed almost no cash to leave the country. It was easy to forget that, despite the trappings of democracy, Dubai like the other six emirates that comprised the UAE, was basically a kingdom.

The dinner was everything he had anticipated and more, and the Contact wore a smile of satisfaction as he exited the restaurant. He now looked forward to getting some sleep. It had been a long, tiring flight and he felt fatigue creeping up on him.

Some 2,500 miles away, in Raqqa in the small room where they lived, the only illumination came from the lights outside. Zahi lay staring unseeingly up at the ceiling. Munsiu had just rolled off her and padded to the bathroom. She was vaguely aware of the sound of splashing water as her mind tried to assimilate the last ten minutes. She felt like she had just been raped. Yes, it was her husband, her Munsiu, but their lovemaking had always been slow and gentle and passionate, and she loved the long cuddles and whispered endearments afterwards. What had changed? She didn't understand. Was it the place? Was it her? Zahi couldn't think.

Her husband had just pushed her legs apart and started thrusting. There was something horrible in the way he had taken her roughly, and without any preliminaries. For the first time, Zahi felt that she had been objectified down to a space of a couple of inches of moist flesh. This can't be happening, she thought, and yet she felt the sick reality of it slowly trickling down the insides of her thighs in sticky, slimy lines. Her belly contracted and a gob of bile turned her mouth sour.

She slowly forced it back and her eyes shifted to the bathroom door as she waited for her husband to emerge. After a few minutes he came out and, without speaking a word, lay down and went to sleep. Zahi walked into the bathroom and, suddenly, her legs couldn't bear her weight anymore. Her back made a squeaking sound against the wall as she slid down to the floor and sat staring into nothingness for long minutes before she rose and stepped towards the bucket of water and started to wash herself, her hands moving slowly and robotically at first and then with quick frantic jerks, her movements getting faster and faster.

***

The next morning found the Contact waiting for Captain Lakhvinder (Jolly) Brar at a café on the Dubai creek side. He felt rested and the sun felt good on his bare forearms. It was a pleasure to be sitting outdoors with an iced tea, wearing a short-sleeved tee, after three months of sweaters and goose down jackets back home. The sun's glare did, however, call for a pair of dark shaded Oakley's and he had not forgotten to pack his.

He spotted the Captain stepping nimbly off a motorized dhow and on to the jetty. As the Contact watched the tall figure pick his way through the usual throng of pedestrians, he noted that the Captain was on time for their appointment, no mean feat for someone who lived on a cargo vessel berthed a dozen nautical miles offshore. Going by the noise the wind made as it buffeted the palm fronds lining the creek, the water must have been pretty choppy.

Captain Brar's countenance showed no sign of discomfort as he walked up to the Contact's table. Both men engaged in a bear hug and pounded each other's backs. The waiter scurried over and the Captain opted for a cafe au lait. By the time it arrived, both men were deep in conversation. The Contact listened with growing fascination as he heard details of the Islamic State's oil economy and the Captain's role in it.

The Islamic State's main oil-producing region was in Syria's eastern Deir Ezzor province. The current rate of production flowed between 34,000 to 40,000 barrels a day, which was being impacted by US-led coalition and Russian airstrikes against its installations. In addition to this, the Islamic State also controlled the Qayyara oil field near Mosul in northern Iraq, and that kicked out around 8,000 barrels a day of heavy oil that was mostly consumed locally. Most oil fields in the area were depleted and the IS did not have the technology or equipment needed to maintain them. The general impression was that the IS relied on exports for its oil revenue, but in actuality it profited from sales to its captive markets closer to home in the rebel-held territories of northern Syria, eastern territories held by the Syrian Kurdish militia and within its own territory straddling the border between Syria and Iraq.

The Islamic State had put in place a precise and coordinated transportation system to sell the oil they siphoned off all the wells they controlled. This included drawing the oil at source and transporting it via a relay of tankers to various ports of distribution, from where it was either auctioned in batches or delivered to an eager bunch of buyers, eager because the IS sold it at a price that undercut the going international rate by 30 per cent. Who could resist such prices? And after all, oil was oil.

Most of its crude oil is sold directly to independent traders at the oil fields. Syrian and Iraqi buyers go directly to the oil fields with their tankers and trucks to buy crude oil. Initially, this used to result in miles-long queues waiting for weeks, but since airstrikes against oil vehicles intensified, the delivery/collection system had been revamped. Currently, when the truckers register outside the field and pick up their number in line, they are told exactly what time they can return to fill up to avoid a pile-up of vehicles and make a more obvious target for strikes. The site managers would collect the crude oil in large pits from where truckers would then fill up. These collection areas often caught fire during air strikes. To make up for lost profits, the IS has tried offering traders a 'licence' that allowed them to jump the queue and get 1,000 barrels of oil at a go, as long as they can pay the entire cost up front and this had been met with partial success. The refineries produced both petrol, and 'mazut'—a heavy form of diesel used in generators that were an absolute necessity as most areas had little or no electricity. Since the quality of the petrol varied widely, and was way more expensive, mazut was in greater demand.

Despite most of the oil being transported overland, crossing several international borders, there was a considerable amount that was delivered on the high seas.

Captain Brar then proceeded to explain. 'The company that I work for has its tankers registered in Panama, which means that the true ownership is hidden beneath multiple layers of shell companies. Once I get my sailing orders, I usually start from Fujairah or Sharjah or Khorfakkan, depending on where I am berthed. All our tankers and bulk carriers are monitored by the Spider web monitoring system, which keeps tabs on each vessel's movement. On a routine run of this sort, my 'on record' destination is Malta, for which I need to pass through the Suez Canal.' The Captain's keen, eyes seemed to gaze back at the route he described.

'I take the UAE-Red Sea-Suez route and proceed towards the Syrian coastline. Now, here is where it gets interesting, some genius has tweaked the monitoring system in a way that it shows my vessel en route to Malta, when in reality, I have diverted course. I get a satellite phone call giving me coordinates and I steer for that until I come across a single-point mooring system about 25 to 35 nautical miles in international waters.'

'What's that? Single-point mooring, you said?' the Contact asked.

'Well, to put it in layman's terms, it's basically a mobile platform which serves as a loading point since it hosts a pipeline that has been extended from the shore.'

'That far? How?' The Contact tried to picture the rig-up.

'The pipeline is extended by towing it seaward, and the oil is pumped by using a relay of booster pumps. The end of the pipeline, which is at the mooring platform, has a manifold system that allows auto-closing.' Captain Brar used a ballpoint to draw a rough diagram on a paper napkin to illustrate his description. The Contact made a mental note to read up on the mooring system and pipeline manifolds. 'You see, what happens is that they drag the pipe to my vessel and commence pumping oil into my cargo holds. It's a bit slow, but in about 24 hours, I usually take in 50,000 barrels. Not bad, eh?' the Captain grinned.

'There is sometimes a line of ships there, and we have to take on armed guards during loading. The last time I picked up cargo was just off the Baniyas coast. These guys are pretty mobile so no two loading points are ever really the same, so it's pretty difficult to detect unless you have the exact coordinates.'

The Contact mulled over what he had just learned. He knew that the Captain was paid three times the going rate for his labours and an additional bonus as 'hazard allowance'. The crew was similarly rewarded. Another year of this, and the Captain intended to retire and spend his days sipping margaritas—no doubt on some sun-kissed beach.

'And the return trip?' the Contact asked Captain Brar.

'I return the same way that I come. The papers of my supposed trip to Malta are doctored, and so are the invoices. I return to the UAE coast with oil procured at way below par, and then it is siphoned off my ship to smaller vessels, after which it is "integrated" into the market—and everybody is smiling on the way to the bank.'

The Captain paused to clear his throat, and the Contact looked at him quizzically. Brar cleared his throat again and said, 'In this connection there is something I wanted to bounce off you, maybe you can help.' The Contact nodded encouragingly.

'I have heard that there is a lookout notice issued for some of my colleagues who have made a few trips too many in this sector. Could you find out about that? It could be the Interpol or some sort of "person of interest" thing, so....' the captain's voice tapered off.

The Contact nodded once more. 'Give me the names and let me ask around and see what I find. So, where do you think you could pick up my cargo?'

The Captain reached into his jacket and pulled out a neatly folded nautical map. He opened and spread it on the table. Both men hunched closer and the Captain started talking once more. An hour later, the two men parted, the Contact walked into the city while the Captain strolled back towards the wharf, his fingers appreciatively caressing a rather plump envelope in his trouser pocket.

The Contact returned to the service apartment. His next meeting wasn't till later in the evening. He lay in the large bed thinking about the man he would meet, a man whose role, if things panned out the way they should, would be a crucial one.

He had first met Dilawar Choudhary on board a Boeing 777 idling in the remote parking bay of an airport just outside of London. The Contact was handling the secure transfer of 50 Afghan detainees back to Kabul and the prisoners were being escorted from a bus that was parked a few feet away from the stepladder. Two securitymen from the delivering firm would help each detainee up the ladder with his hands cuffed behind his back. At the door of the aircraft the Contact and two guards stood ready to take custody. The detainee was turned around, his handcuffs swiftly removed and exchanged for a pair of wire cuffs, after which he was walked to his seat in the aircraft where his feet were secured. He would stay there for the duration of the voyage except for a single toilet break, during which he would be escorted back and forth by a guard on either side of him. The escort guards were big beefy men and were unarmed. In fact, only six men, including the Contact, carried weapons. They were Glock 17s, with a third of the powder removed from the cartridges for obvious reasons. Firing inside an aircraft 30,000 feet above ground wasn't a good idea at any time. The Contact had drilled his security team repeatedly until they had got it down to an art form. He stood a few steps inside the aircraft, closely supervising each custody transfer. One detainee made a break for it at the time of switching cuffs but the guards quickly and efficiently subdued him, forcing him face down to a prone position. The guy had started screaming in a language the Contact had not heard at the time. One of the guards started speaking to the detainee in what evidently was the same language who eventually stopped his hysterical screaming. Afterwards, the Contact had taken the guard aside and asked him about his conversation with the detainee. It emerged that the guard named Dilawar Choudhary spoke Pashtu, which was the dominant language in Afghanistan. Dilawar's mother was Pashtu-born and the family had since shifted to Oman. The Contact asked him a few more questions about his background and experience and had come away impressed with the compactly built, bearded man with swarthy skin and knowledge of half a dozen Middle-Eastern dialects. The Contact had kept in touch with him, and in the years that followed, they had worked together on a couple of assignments and developed a mutual professional respect in addition to forming the unique bond that friendship between mercenaries results in. Currently, Dilawar ran a profitable business trading in spices and grain with a neat sideline in smuggling contraband in and out of areas of conflict under the guise of trading in scrap metal. Dilawar Choudhary was a man of many enterprises.

The evening found the Contact sitting at a veranda table of the Beachcombers restaurant at the Jumeirah hotel on Al Wasl Road. He liked the restaurant, in equal measure, for the Pan-Asian menu that included an incredible Malay chicken rendang curry, as well as the view it offered of the dhow-shaped Hotel Burj al Arab and the water beyond. The Contact was the first to arrive and he selected a table that afforded privacy. A few minutes later, Dilawar arrived and the two men shook hands in delight. They had not met for three years and the stocky spice trader was quick to point out that the Contact seemed to have lost some bulk. According to him, that owed itself to the absence of a wife and he offered to send a list of names and photographs to the Contact so that he could remedy the matter with a woman of his choice. They were all good women, he assured the Contact. Why, Dilawar himself would vouch for each and every one of them!

The Contact politely refused the proffered assistance with a poker-face while his friend grinned mischievously at his obvious discomfort. The Contact in turn enquired about Dilawar's many wives and mistresses and the spice trader with twinkling eyes assured him that all of them were happy and contented in every sense of the word. The banter and ripostes back and forth continued over the first drink but as soon as the waitress brought them their first refill, both men got down to the business of the day.

'I have an operation going in the Syria-Turkey theatre,' began the Contact. 'It's not the usual hit-and-run kind of thing and I need to do an extraction. It's a female and she will actively assist,' the Contact said.

He then looked into Dilawar's eyes. 'She is in an as yet undetermined location in Raqqa, my friend. I very much need to execute this one, it's personal.'

'Personal?' The spice trader's eyebrows rose in support of his query.

'Yes, she is the sister of an old friend and was lured there under a false pretext.' The Contact outlined the entire sequence of events within minutes. He needed this man's total confidence and the only way to get that was by telling him the whole unadulterated truth. The spice trader punctuated the Contact's narrative with nods and shakes of his head. His was a traditional Muslim household in the Gulf, and he understood only too well the young girl's predicament. At length the Contact stopped, and reached for a sip of his single malt. 'Do you have any assets or business in Islamic State territory?' he asked bluntly.

'My dear man, I have businesses everywhere!' Dilawar laughed. 'I do run a tidy line in supplies to most of the players there—except the Iranian lot, them I don't trust, bloody Shias.' He paused for a moment, apparently reconsidering his statement. 'Well, a few of them are good, I suppose, the ones I do business with, that is,' his eyes twinkled again.

The Contact laughed with his friend. Dilawar was an unscrupulous rascal but an amiable one, and fiercely loyal to his friends—and heaven knew that he himself was in no position to pass judgement on anyone, not after the things he had done.

'What is your range of activities over there?' the Contact asked.

'Oh, scrap metal, grain, spices, tinned household stuff, electrical, cigarettes, tobacco, medical supplies, you know, the usual,' Dilawar said idly. 'There is a growing line in refugee-smuggling and transportation, particularly after that Sinjar and Yazidi thing.'

The Contact nodded his comprehension.

The Islamic State had swept across northern Iraq's Sinjar region and on the 3rd of August, invaded the town of the same name. Those of the ancient Yazidi minority had particular reason to fear the invaders. Their religion, Yazidism, is linked to ancient Mesopotamian religions and combines aspects of Zoroastrianism, Islam, Christianity and Judaism. The Islamic State considers the sect heretical, and its followers, devil-worshippers, who were be captured, converted, or executed.

IS soldiers came in the early hours, a large force armed with weapons plundered from the Iraqi army. They advanced swiftly through the darkness and encountered little resistance from the Iraqi Kurdish Peshmerga fighters, who had retreated in panic and disarray, leaving the citizens unprotected. Men, women and children made a dash for the nearby Sinjar mountain by whatever means of transportation that would take them as close as possible to the jagged ridge, as small groups of poorly equipped local men fought a desperate rear-guard battle to block the road and buy time to save their families.

Others weren't quick or lucky enough to follow, and the Islamic State's soldiers slaughtered entire villages, killing at least 5,000 Yazidi men and boys, and abducting as many as 7,000 women and girls as sex slaves. In the subsequent months, the women and minor girls were sold and resold, even auctioned in sex-slave markets.

Since then, some of the stories that emerged from Sinjar were even more horrific, and according to Dilawar, there were now groups actively involved in tracing and rescuing the Yazidi women and minor girls. Many a time, smugglers, with their contacts and knowledge of the terrain, were instrumental in these rescues and the going rate for such assignments was in the region of 40,000 US dollars. And yet, thought the Contact, Sinjar was in Iraq, and Raqqa was in Syria. While there were commonalities in both situations the fact remained that Sinjar was in a state of flux with several players and the ever-changing dynamics of territorial supremacy, and Raqqa was firmly under the dominion of the Islamic State.

Both men were silent for a while, Dilawar looking at but no seeing the water and the brilliantly lit ultra-luxurious Burj al Arab hotel with its distinctive shape and the Contact's gaze running over the restaurant's interior as the tables started filling up and the staff suddenly becoming busier. The waitress looked over and then approached their table once again; the men elected for another refill and regarded each other pensively. They were aware of the issues involved, should they come to an understanding and a decision. As covert operations went, this would be right on top of the risk matrix and any sort of failure would mean a messy and painful end with a body or two rotting in an undignified heap on a pile of garbage, with dogs gnawing at it, or sprawled on some inhospitable terrain awaiting the attentions of maggots and other carrion-eaters as the cells putrefied and the skin blistered. They had been at such scenes before and every experience chipped away at the armour of their courage and fortitude.

The Contact finally broke the silence. 'Well, what do you think?'

The spice trader raised his shoulders till they were near his ears and held them there for a few seconds before dropping them again and said, 'It's doable, I suppose, if she is capable and if we get all the parts very right including the timing and location and a dozen more things and ifs.' He looked across at the man he held in such high esteem and considered his friend. As Allah is my witness, he thought, this one can make me walk on burning coals, for he commands all my respect and affection, and there is this strange energy that I feel when I am around him.

So, with the madness that takes over all warriors at times, Dilawar smiled and said, 'Boy, if we can pull this one off.... '

The spice trader's smile revealed two rows of gleaming white teeth as he reached out and grabbed the Contact by his left arm and squeezed it, and the Contact smiled back in pure relief because now he wouldn't have to go to an unknown and hence unreliable source, and because he had just saved his friend a shitload of money that another outfit would demand, and mostly and above all, because Dilawar was in and that was all that mattered now.

'The best way is by road to the coastline, and then by sea.' Dilawar had his elbows on the table and was peering down at his cell phone. He had a map of the Syrian coast on his screen. 'It's about 425 km from Raqqa to the coast, give or take a few kilometres,' Dilawar said in a low monotone. The Contact knew that he was thinking aloud.

'It would mean a 7-to-8-hour trip overland with multiple checkpoints and a rendezvous with a boat,' Dilawar concluded. 'I could arrange both,' he continued. 'There would be separate teams, and I would be there myself to supervise and troubleshoot.' Both men knew that the spice trader would automatically double his exposure to danger this way.

'I can handle the next part, my friend,' the Contact said. 'It would be safer for you and, besides, I need the exercise.' Both men grinned and Dilawar nodded in acquiescence,

'She needs to travel light and I need to have authentication,' Dilawar warned.

The Contact nodded. 'I will arrange that,' he said. He knew exactly what his friend meant. Zahi would need to be certain who she was meeting up with and more importantly, have confidence in

Dilawar. Without that the whole thing could go south very fast.

An hour later the Contact was heading back to his service apartment. He would get a good night's sleep before catching an afternoon flight to Mumbai, India.

CHAPTER TWELVE

The green, yellow and blue strings of beads—perhaps twenty of them—that hung vertically from the door frame served as a curtain. They also effectively separated the small grocery with its motley collection of fruits, soft drinks, snacks and knick-knacks from the larger room that housed the Internet café. Zahi and her sisters-in-law had picked up a couple of bottles of water and a few bags of peanuts before sweeping aside the strings and entering the café. As they stepped in, the beads swung back into place with several click-clacks and then hung silently once more. The café had about 10 computers and the room was stiflingly hot despite the twin rows of pedestal fans that whirred noisily in an effort to cool both the desktop terminals as well as the customers.

There was another entrance to the café: one could directly walk in from the street outside by pushing open a glass-panelled door that advertised the Casbah Internet café and purchase surfing time at the counter. You paid the equivalent of 3 US dollars for an hour on one of the computers. Zahi and the others were on a supervised visit as this was their first time, and Marium, a sour-faced, middle-aged spinster from the Al Khansaa Brigade, accompanied them.

The brigade was formed in early 2014 and is named after Al Khansa, a woman poet from the earlier days of

Islam. It is unique in the Muslim world, since in other regimes with similar systems of religious police, such as Saudi Arabia, it is men that enforce 'hisbah' among women. The Islamic State had introduced the brigade in Mosul and Raqqa, and women of Al Khansaa sometimes carried weapons and participated in firefights. Women in the Islamic State are normally prohibited from (except under special dispensation) carrying arms or driving. but the Al Khansaa can do both. These were generally women hailing from Western countries, those who may have had military or law-enforcement training, and were usually more robust physically. The Al Khansaa cadets underwent a 60-day 'training and religious refresher course' before being assigned duties.

Women who go out without a male chaperone or aren't fully covered in public were liable to be arrested and subjected to punitive beatings by Al-Khansaa. There were regulations to be enforced even in the context of social and public behaviour, and it wasn't unusual for a woman to receive up to 20 lashes for wearing form-fitting abayas or for wearing makeup underneath their veils. There were other affiliated punishments such as 10 lashes for 'not displaying an appropriate amount humility or meekness' when stopped for questioning.

Zahi and the others opted for a single terminal and sat in a group on plastic chairs. Marium hovered over them, preferring to stand. Owners of the Internet café could not operate without obtaining a licence from the local Islamic State communications office and part of the terms and conditions of the licence stipulated that the owners had to monitor and report any suspicious activity by any of its customers. Since the IS did not encourage or allow operating an independent Internet system, all routers were under its supervision and subject to vigilance. Several cafés had been recently shut down after it was found that their owners were providing net access to nearby residents. In spite of this, many people used private cell phones with Internet capability although they had to be very careful. Even the suspicion of being a spy or a security risk could invite summary execution.

As a security measure there were specially equipped minivans that roamed the more crowded localities to trace and pinpoint independent Internet usage and providers. These had advanced WiFi detectors brought in from Turkey to catch violators. Another imperative the Islamic State faced in this connection was the need to combat misinformation and propaganda. There was the recent case of the security office arresting people in Raqqa and its countryside for possessing satellite internet dongles distributed by Smart News, a pro-rebel Syrian website.

Zahi typed in her password and accessed her email for the first time in weeks. She wasn't allowed to write to anyone, not yet, and she had made the single call to her mother in the presence of Munsiu. Her mother had been weepy and hysterical in turns but had finally calmed down sufficiently to ask a few questions. There was little that Zahi could tell her in Munsiu's presence and even if he hadn't been there, she had been instructed by her brother Ahmed to keep conversation limited to everyday topics and on no account talk about the other phone and their regular texts. Once Zahi had learned about the roving security vans with the capability to detect telecommunications and Internet activities she had kept her phone usage to the strict minimum. It was clear to her by then that it wasn't just dangerous but downright suicidal to be caught engaging in unauthorized communications.

The menfolk had left for three weeks of training that was to be followed by some field exercises in the countryside, and the women were more or less confined to the house they had been allotted a fortnight ago, a two-level, four-bedroom structure. They had been told that the family would be allowed cell phones after the men returned from their training, but Zahara and Zoona had already sweet-talked one of the women in the neighbourhood to allow them the use of her cell phone, and made a call to their mother a week ago. Her three sisters-in-law seemed perfectly at ease with the multitude of restrictions imposed on their movements and lifestyle. Zahi, in her misery, thought that they seemed to almost welcome it. She was now quite sure that it had been the women who had prevailed upon their brothers into making the move to migrate to the nascent caliphate. Obviously, Zoona's and Lena's husbands would never have agreed, so they had to be left behind. Zahara's husband would follow her anywhere, he was so totally besotted by her. Zahi had spent considerable time thinking about the depth and force of motivation and religious conviction in play that would make young, married women with children come happily away to this hellhole of a place, in response to an archaic and dubious call to arms against an entire world of perceived heretics and idolaters.

Zahi had not been surprised at the exclusion of her eldest and, as far as she was concerned, dearest brother-in-law Sameer, the gentle doctor with the kind eyes and soft voice. Had he an inkling of his siblings' intention, he would never have allowed the family to leave the country and head into this madness. She wondered how he felt now. She dragged her mind to the present and forced herself to scroll through her mail hurriedly, so that the others could have their turn. Ten minutes later, she had finished and sat back in the chair, sipping at her orange pop. With the menfolk gone from the house, she was forced to be extra careful while using her phone. Her sisters-in-law were prone to barging into her room without even knocking on the door. She continued to use the bathroom for her texts. Zahi's thoughts often strayed to her brother's friend, the one who was going to get her out. Who was he? She wondered what manner of a man he was. Surely, a decent man, to have agreed to help. Zahi was suddenly aware that the Al Khansaa woman Marium was staring at her and she instinctively forced a smile to her face. Allah! I hate this woman, she thought. As

Zahi pretended to watch the others at the computer terminal, her mind drifted away to a place of solitude in search of a tiny measure of peace.

***

The brothers Aabir and Munsiu, and their brother-in-law Qassim, had travelled in a white minibus with ten others to a basic training camp at the Omar oilfield in the desert of Mayadin, Deir Ezzor, in eastern Syria. The training-in-charge, a heavy-built fierce-looking Chechen, received them on arrival and showed them to the lodgings where they would spend the next few weeks. The training of recruits ranged from a month upto a year, depending on what roles they were earmarked for. Inside the camps, students received a mix of military, political and Sharia orientation, usually delivered by around five instructors. The military component stressed on handling of semi-automatic to fully automatic weapons, mainly Kalashnikovs and the vehicle-mounted machine-guns. Those with former military experience and showing special aptitude were selected for sniper training. A degree in chemical or mechanical engineering meant that the student could be steered toward the explosive ordnance section, or towards innovation-led sections such as drone technology, making vehicle-borne improvised explosive devices (IEDs) or chemicals used in bio-warfare. Students of a more scholarly bent of mind were groomed for the activities of the Sharia council.

Recruits were occasionally dispatched to checkpoints as part of their field exercises, but not to the frontlines. There was extra emphasis on field craft and urban guerrilla warfare tactics, and the making of crude, IEDs.

After graduation, newbies remained under supervision for about four months and were liable to be expelled or punished in case of instances of noncompliance, or if they expressed reservations. In some cases, those who were more squeamish about, or had difficulty in, participating in some aspects of the brutalities of the Islamic State's tactics, were sent back to receive more training to 'fortify' their faith.

All recruits were first taught the basics about religion; the intention was a cleansing of religious innovations and Ba'athist ideas. An oft-repeated lesson was that issuance of fatwas was restricted to clerics, and nobody could kill without a fatwa, unless in the battlefield. There were also tutorials in Arabic, and the recruits learned how to speak in standard Arabic if they did not already know.

The IS depends heavily on what Muslim clerics consider isolated incidents described in sacred texts that they believed should not be followed as rules. The merits of such incidents are touted to bolster a doctrinal idea. The IS uses transpose: these instances to help members who struggle with issues such as hesitation in carrying out acts like decapitation or some other brutality. When these stories were weaved into the overall ideology of the Islamic State, new members found it easier to accept them.

Because the Islamic State's training strategy bases its teachings on those religious texts that mainstream Muslim clerics skirt around, or avoid dealing with head-on, new recruits leave the training camp feeling that they have finally arrived at the true meaning and message of Islam. The younger the student, the easier and more effective was the indoctrination. Recruits therefore graduated armed with theological arguments, military training and a conviction that other Muslims are at least partly complicit in the suppression of true Islam, in addition to the distinct feeling that they had been misled before. This exponentially increased their new-found religious fervour.

Aabir took to the training like the proverbial duck to water, his slim young body easily coping with the physical regimen. He excelled at the obstacle course and in unarmed combat. Since he hadn't been very religious to begin with, and had scant knowledge of the Koran and the Arabic texts, his brain was like a sponge that eagerly and rapidly soaked up everything his tutors and the Islamic State clerics had to offer. Munsiu, on the other hand, had never been the athletic type. His somewhat pudgy body was clumsy on the training course and he struggled with most of the physical curriculum. The two brothers couldn't have been more different and their training continued under the keen eyes of the trainers who were constantly watching and evaluating each recruit for strengths and potential flaws. It was Qassim that was the surprise. The calm, quiet Qassim, who was so devoted to his wife Zahara, the short slim mechanical engineer Qassim with his flair for energizing even the most recalcitrant of motors, had proven to be a natural soldier and equally attentive and devoted to the teachings of the clerics. In the weeks that followed Qassim quickly earned the respect of both brothers and his fellow trainees.

***

The Contact was in Mumbai. It was a city that never ceased to amaze him with its abundance of energies. Everyone seemed to be working an angle, and the objective was usually money or fame, though preferably both, but it was also a city where the anonymous remained in the shadows where they were at home, plying their secret trades and yet hiding in plain sight.

He had landed at the Chhatrapati Shivaji International airport a little past noon, and had checked into the Orchid. A light meal was followed by a brief phone call to confirm Raoul Miranda's availability. An hour later, he was in a private taxi that the travel desk at the hotel had rustled up on his request.

The pretty young thing at the reception desk pressed a button on the intercom and the door to Miranda's cabin clicked open. The Contact stepped in and both men clasped hands. Raoul offered a cup of tea which the Contact politely turned down, opting instead for a glass of water. Frequent flying tended to mildly dehydrate him and so he compensated. The glass of cold water arrived and he was pleased to see a slice of lemon floating in it. He smiled his thanks to the pretty receptionist and both men waited until she left the room.

'What happened to the last one?' the Contact asked.

'Oh, I replace them every few months,' the big man replied. 'It's good for me and good for the business.'

The Contact nodded in understanding. A sharp receptionist was bound to notice and remember things after a period of time. And a regular turnover of staff made for good security in Raoul's business. He watched as the man opened a safe box set into the wall next to his desk and took out a brown envelope. Raoul tossed it on the desk and the Contact reached over and picked it up. The flap was held shut by a couple of paperclips and he eased them off. Opening the envelope, he slid the contents out, one by one, and inspected the documents.

The passport was the largest, there wasn't any doubt about the genuineness; it was an authentic Indian passport and could pass all visual and electronic scrutiny. Only, it had started as a blank passport, one of a small batch that found its way to Raoul Miranda. It had lain in a safe place until such time that it had to take on an identity. Now it had a photograph, a name and all the entry and exit stamps of a moderately travelled person. The travel history went back three years and the passport itself was five years old.

The Contact riffled through the pages until he came to a week-old entry stamp. The page also carried a three-month validity tourist visa for that country. The Contact recognized that the passport had actually travelled out and then probably was returned by courier. He didn't ask Raoul and he didn't want to know. What mattered was the document.

He then turned his attention to the other documents. There was a driving licence, an Adhaar card proving Indian national identity, a debit and a credit card and an old college identity tag. Raoul had even included an ATM withdrawal slip and the stubs of two old cinema tickets. All the documents appeared used and well 'aged'. The Contact then came upon a slip of paper with a series of names and some alphanumeric sequences. He raised his eyebrows at Raoul, who said, 'I opened up a Facebook account in the name and populated it a bit. The other numbers are ATM pin codes and the one at the end is the sample signature used for all applications and bank records.'

Raoul continued, 'I will keep adding to the social media profile till such time you as you tell me otherwise.'

The Contact nodded in appreciation. This was why he favoured Raoul Miranda. He was expensive but you got the best. If it came to it, Raoul could supply all the other documentation that a person required to be an Indian citizen. He was worth every penny.

'You can carry everything but the passport in your luggage, and have an explanation for it,' Raoul informed him. 'May I suggest a possible solution to any problems you may foresee in regard to the second passport?

'Of course,' the Contact replied. He had planned to buy a suitably thick hardbound with a dust jacket. He would have removed the jacket, placed the passport inside, and used a strong adhesive to glue the two together, so that the passport didn't slip out. But he was always ready to listen to another professional.

Raoul pulled open a drawer in his desk and took out something. He handed it over to the Contact who saw that it was a passport-holder with multiple sleeves for tickets, boarding passes, visiting cards, currency and such. He looked across at Raoul, who grinned and said, 'You will notice the extra pocket in the inner sleeve.'

The Contact looked closely into the holder and found a recessed sleeve held closed by a very thin strip of velcro. 'Just place the passport in there,' Raoul continued, 'and carry it on you with your own passport. Even if it shows up on the baggage-screener there will be no reason to arouse suspicion, it will be taken for an old passport.'

The Contact thought about it. Yes, it made perfect sense and even if a thoroughly invasive search was made for any reason, he stood a fair chance of talking his way out of it. It would be a different kettle of fish if the search unearthed the passport concealed in the book jacket. He decided to keep the passport-holder.

The Contact replaced everything inside the envelope, stood up and shook hands with Raoul again. 'I will transfer an extra something to the account,' he said. 'There may be some further need. Thanks, this is really good work.'

'Always a pleasure,' the big man replied and walked the Contact to the door. A final nod and the Contact left. He had to fly back to Dubai, where there was just transpose: one small thing to do before he returned home.

CHAPTER THIRTEEN

New York, United States

Mark Ross sat at his desk and studied the cell phone activity reports, all seven of them. When the Contact had given him the list of SIM numbers, he had put them on an electronic intel watchlist as a matter of routine. In fact, he had almost forgotten about them, when suddenly, all the numbers had come to life on Saturday evening US east coast time. The Elint guys had only just sent the packet over and he had seen the email alert as soon as he logged in after the weekend. The delay wasn't damaging, but nevertheless, he made a mental note to tell them to flag everything related to this case as urgent and dispatch it immediately, regardless of day and time. The CDR (call detail record) indicated that all the cell phones were currently in the same area so it was likely that the family was together at present, if, that is, it was indeed family using the SIMs. He would have to ask the Contact to confirm and connect the names with the numbers.

Mark drew a deep breath. This was a great development, the ability to triangulate and track the individuals, especially the Pilot. He pecked away at the keyboard, putting in a requisition for call interceptions on all the numbers. This meant that the Elint team would have to figure out the best way to tap into the calls made to and from the numbers, so that they would be recorded, and then a translator would transcribe each conversation. The requisition also covered text messages and other activity.

The languages department was going to freak out over this one. Mark grinned at the thought of them scrambling for... what was the Maldivian language called?... yes, 'Dwivehi', they would have to scramble to find a Dwivehi-speaking translator who had a top-secret security clearance. Mark grinned again, imagining the flurry of activity his requisition would generate.

Scrolling down the email, he noted that several of the email addresses that the Contact had provided had also shown activity. The guys from cyber forensics had dispatched a seemingly random advertisement which was actually an email tracker in disguise, and that had bounced back results. The IP address was shown as somewhere in Iraq, but he was sure it was a fake one, generated by a dynamic IP address-generating software. The team at forensics would keep chipping away at it until they were successful in backtracking through the maze of servers and codes designed to thwart tracing the physical location of the computer. Sometimes, they were successful. At other times....

Despite the major and continuous advances in spyware technology, and what was touted in films, cell phone communication interception was still an iffy thing and had its limitations. Also, it could be thwarted or defended against. The FBI, and other law enforcement agencies, use a range of devices made by the Harris Corporation. The most widely used of these are the Stingray, and the handheld Kingfisher, to track people's movements, and intercept and record conversations, contact listed numbers and text messages from mobile phones. Typically, using a Stingray entails the monitoring and collection of data from all mobile phones within a specific target area. A Stingray is often used in combination with portable 'Hailstorm towers' that jam the mobile phone signals in a limited area, forcing phones to drop down from 4G and 3G network bands to older, less secure, 2G bands. This increases the quality of the access because hacking is easier at lower bandwidths.

In situations such as the current one, when placing of a Stingray was clearly not possible, other techniques were explored. One possibility was getting Zahi to place a cell phone bug. These can be implemented by disabling the ringing feature on a mobile phone, thereby allowing a caller to call that phone to access its microphone and listen in. Intentionally hiding a cell phone in a location is a widely used bugging technique, but the key element was managing to hide the cell phone in a place that guaranteed maximum intelligence. Other cell phone bugs relied on wifi hotspots, rather than cellular data, where the tracker root kit software can be programmed to 'wake up' at predicated times and sign into a public wifi hotspot to upload tracker data onto a public Internet server.

The FBI also used 'roving bugs', which entails the activation of microphones on mobiles to enable the monitoring of conversations, but to a trained person, there are many defences to such interceptions. The most common one is just disconnecting the microphone from the circuit board, or lacking that expertise, simply using a needle and a ball-peen hammer to smash the microphone and using a Bluetooth or external plug-in while making calls.

Mark was aware that even a very moderately trained person can easily detect signs of electronic surveillance, such as a mobile phone waking up unexpectedly, or an inordinate increase in CPU usage while on idle or not in use. Other positive indicators of surveillance are the hearing of clicking or beeping sounds when conversations occur, and the circuit board of the phone getting warm despite the phone not being used. To an observant individual, such symptoms are dead giveaways.

Therefore, any person can take preventive measures against unwelcome electronic access by simple actions such as keeping the phone switched off and then removing the battery when not in use. Another simple solution would be to use an improvised Faraday pouch to carry the cell phone. One can also just insert random thin metal wires, tinfoil and a few metal scraps or plates, thereby reducing the possibility of remote access to a minimum.

The more the FBI agent thought over the problem, he was increasingly convinced that the best solution was to insert a software into all the target cell phones via a 'Spore'. They would disguise the spyware in maybe a picture or an emoticon, and then monitor it remotely. This would allow observation of the target cell phones' geographical location in real-time on a map, and enable microphones to capture and forward conversations during a call. In addition to this, the team would receive remote alerts or text messages each time somebody dialled a number on the targetted cell phone.

The Elint team's biggest problem would be the file size of the 'Spore'; too big and it would attract suspicion, too light and it would limit actions. Well, he told himself, we'll sort that out somehow, as he reached for the phone. A meeting with the Contact was now imperative.

Malé

Muzzafar Salim of the Maldives police (Sensitive and Confidential Unit) was also sitting at his desk and he too was poring over call detail records. There were three of them, to be precise, and pertained to Dr Sameer Ibraheem, Ahmed Idris and Idris's wife. The decision to betray a friendship of many years' standing had come surprisingly easily to Salim. They had grown up together, indeed they had gone to the same school and their parents had been friends too. While Idris had enlarged his father's business, Salim had chosen to enlist in the Maldives police department, and promotions had been slow. At forty-five he was a mid-level police officer relegated to being in charge of a unit that just kept its ear to the ground on the off chance that some anti-government chatter or activity might be detected. Salim was very much aware that his unit was more of a tool to subdue the political opposition and other social media activists and liberals.

Apart from the fact that he had always resented Idris's designer clothes, his posh office and his pretty wife, Salim was a man of orthodox thought. While Ahmed Idris went to Europe to pursue a college education and Sameer studied to be a doctor, Salim had attended two years of religious studies in Saudi Arabia. The Salaf had extended him a scholarship and the resultant stint had deeply engraved on his mind the merits of Salafi traditions and ideology.

The Salaf had started off as a minor NGO that had been registered in the Maldives after the tsunami. Its finances originated from Kuwait and it still remained an NGO in form, although its dimensions and nature of activities had over the years subtly morphed into something very different. It was through the Salaf that the Saudi Salafi clerics introduced Salafi Wahhabism into the Maldives. Islanders in far off atolls who had suffered financial deprivations in the tsunami's aftermath, were told that the disaster was the consequence of people's departure from the true meaning of Islam. The NGO's activities, like religious scholarships and 'life skills' coaching camps, thereafter started gaining appreciation and slowly became popular. Today, the Salaf was both a religious and political force that helped keep the president in power. Its local head, Shaik Adnan Shakil, had recently been elevated to the Fathwa Majlis, the supreme Islamic council of the country. Shaikh Adnan and Muzzafar Salim had been classmates in Kuwait and the future had suddenly brightened up for the policeman.

Salim's memory flashed back to his last meeting and conversation with Idris. Who was this 'friend' that Idris said was in the UK or was it the US? What was his background and why did Idris think he could help? Salim was uncomfortably aware that increasing attention was being focused on the Maldives as a hotbed of radicalization, particularly in the context of recruitment by the Islamic State and Al-Qaeda. If one looked at the percentage of the population of the Maldives that left their families and homeland in order to fight in the jihad, the Maldives had the highest percentage of radicalization. The government officially owned up to 50 or 60 persons leaving the country to join the Islamic State, but Salim knew the real figure was closer to 300 and rising. In fact, some Maldivians were reportedly engaged in fighting alongside the Jabhat al Nusra, which was an Al-Qaeda affiliate in Iraq and Syria, which meant that there were Maldivians fighting against each other in that theatre of war.

The policeman turned his attention back to the call details, his cursor ran to the day after the family had left for Turkey. Let's see, he thought, whom did Ahmed Idris call that day? The cursor stopped at a call late that evening that Idris had made to a US number. Salim highlighted the number and pasted it on for a 'frequency' search in the CDR analysis software. There were no more calls to that number from Idris's phone. The policeman ran a check on the other two call details and the number did not reflect in either. Was this the mysterious 'friend'? The policeman decided to dig further and made a few calls. In an hour he had an address, a photograph and a passport number. A quick check with the Maldives immigration desk showed that the person concerned had visited the Maldives several times before. Another hour of probing revealed several more facts, all of them disturbing, and the policeman scribbled notes as the information came in, piece by piece. And why were there no more calls to this obviously capable friend, wondered Salim. Were they using Facebook or Telegram or any of the dozens of social media applications to communicate? Did they email each other? There was only one way to find out....

Finally, Muzzafar Salim sat back in his chair, his right thumb absently rubbing the leather on his armrest in a slow circular action. He considered the findings of the last two hours and the single-most obvious fact was that Ahmed Idris had done nothing illegal, but the policeman believed that Idris's actions, combined with his friend's capabilities, had the potential to bring a firestorm into the fluid fight for power currently engulfing the Maldives. While much was known to the state intelligence agencies about the activities of NGOs and religious organizations, nothing had been committed to paper. There was a considerable overlap where state security and religious outreach were concerned, but those were matters that were best laid on the lap of men holding higher stations. The policeman was a dyed-in-the-wool Salafi and his loyalties lay with the Salaf and Shaikh Adnan.

Thus, with no more thought to whatever social unpleasantness might follow as far his relationship with Idris and Sameer was concerned, Muzzafar Salim reached for the phone and dialled the number of his friend Shaikh Adnan Shakil.

Raqqa, Syria

The men were back in the house in Raqqa, the sisters-in-law were delighted, and Zahi felt as if there was a stranger in the room. She had been totally taken aback by the change in Munsiu. He walked with his back rigid. Gone was the natural slouch. Now there was a squarer set to his shoulders. His palms were hard and callused and he looked bigger somehow. The family was able to go out more freely now that the men were accompanying the women, and Zahi felt that there was an appreciable difference in the attitude of neighbours and the township in general. It was as if they had passed some test or trial and now they were all part of a whole. She knew it was because the men had been through training and the whole family was now worthy of being included in the mainstream of the Islamic State's society. The women, including the Al Khansaa, and the suicide squad in the 'caliphate', she had grown to realize, were to consider themselves privileged to be able to participate. Here in Syria, as in the Maldives, nothing seemed to have changed—it was a man's world and men made the rules.

They had all been given permission to have cell phones, the youngster had been enrolled in school, the ration cards had been delivered and Qassim had purchased a car. It was a Toyota Fortuner and the couple had gone on a 'test drive' that had lasted for eighteen hours, something that invited much merriment and innuendoes in the days that followed. Zahi had made a list of the cell phone numbers and the users and texted them to Idris the same night. She now had two cell phones.

Oman

Dilawar Choudhary, the spice trader, was a practical man. He knew that getting someone out of Raqqa was a dangerous venture, but he was also determined to succeed at the task his friend had given him—the money be damned—he owed the man and some debts are impossible to repay. The Contact and he had a history going back a decade and a half, and each man had earned the respect and trust of the other. Dilawar knew his way around Syria, he knew the highways, the unpaved smugglers' routes and the little-known pathways and trails that hugged the coastline. He had traded in almost everything in his time and still did, although now he was greatly assisted by his firstborn, Yasser, a strapping six-footer who worshipped him. As father and son sat under the tree in the courtyard after dinner that night, Dilawar's wife glanced over more than once at the two men she loved more than anyone else in the world. She knew something was up but held her silence because business was business and woman had no part to play in it, and besides, she would come to know eventually, she always did.

'It can be done, Father,' Yasser said, 'the pick-up, I mean. The problem will be the drive across to the coast. Who knows how many checkpoints.... ' his voice trailed off.

'Do we have any outsize cargo coming out of there?' Dilawar asked.

Yasser shook his head. 'Just sheet metal and other scrap, and they check those thoroughly. Besides, those trips always involve at least a dozen men for loading and unloading.' He added, 'And the men always accompany the cargo. It would be impossible to have a woman along and keep it secret.'

Both men pondered over the task. A trek overland on foot, moving only at night, was always an option, Dilawar supposed, but would the woman be up to it? And if they stumbled upon a mobile war party? The resultant firefight would almost certainly involve casualties and the element of secrecy would be lost. He turned to call out to his wife for a cup of coffee when his grandson came running to him and jumped on to his lap. Both men smiled as the toddler tugged at the folds of his robes. Yasser's wife hurried over and led away the protesting little one, admonishing him in a low undertone. They watched mother and child walk across the courtyard and until both disappeared into the house.

The coffee came in steaming cups. Both men stretched out their legs as a wind cooled by the Sea of Oman continued to rustle the leaves overhead.

CHAPTER FOURTEEN

United States

The whole thing landed in a sloppy, shapeless heap and splattered into a yellow and white mess. The Contact grimaced. He had never mastered the art of flipping an omelette and this one lay only partly in the pan with the gooey remnants sputtering up at him in rebuke. He had just finished mopping up the spill from the stovetop when the cell phone rang. It was Mark Ross.

'Hello, is it a good time to talk?' Mark queried.

The Contact glanced at the waiting plate on the table and said, 'Yes, as good as any. Is there any news?'

'Well, not exactly, though there has been a development. Those SIM cards numbers you gave us? Well, some of them got activated.'

'Oh?' The Contact went to his desk and picked up the list that Idris had passed on. 'Are we sure who is operating them?' he asked.

Mark paused. He tended to forget that he was talking to a man who could be termed an experienced operative. 'Well, reasonably sure. They are in the same location, cell tower-wise, we were hoping you could get us confirmation on that, and there were a couple of other things. I think we should meet up today, if that's possible.'

'Fine,' the Contact replied. 'It's 9 right now, so let's say, at noon?'

They decided to meet at a café outside Bryant Park. The Contact walked over and viewed the remains of his omelette, then shrugged and taking two slices of wheat bread and pouring himself a glass of orange juice from the carton in the fridge, sat down to have his breakfast.

Noon saw Mark Ross and Chris Bellamy sitting opposite the Contact in the Green Heron. The Contact began by passing the list of numbers and users to Mark. 'Those are the numbers and the members of the family using them. Zahi sent them last night. We can expect photographs and landmark coordinates now.'

Both agents looked at each other for a moment and Mark said, 'That's great, we are really making progress now, if she can keep us informed as to some specifics then we will be better placed to rescue her.'

'Don't you have any assets in that area?' the Contact asked, his eyes holding Mark's.

The agent replied, 'Well, we are mobilizing them, it may take some time and besides, we do need to coordinate any operations with the coalition forces and local allies on the ground there, as I am sure you can appreciate.' He cleared his throat, 'And the Pilot's location is crucial, of course.'

There was a momentary silence at the table and the Contact mulled over the exchange so far. What was being *unsaid* was: 'No pilot, no rescue.' The US agencies weren't worried about a family of half a dozen who had gone to fight for the Islamic State's caliphate, they were naturally concerned about the danger a pilot trained in the United States posed in terms of another terrorist strike and its aftermath. Where Zahi and her utility were concerned the intelligence agencies would milk the cow as enthusiastically as they would slaughter it. One more body in a hijab and headscarf buried in a collapsed structure wasn't likely to tilt the balance one way or the other.

The Contact directly addressed Mark again. 'Well, now that we have the numbers live, you guys will need to map out the activity of each of them. So, do you have the software patch ready for me?' He smiled.

There he's done it again, thought Mark, he's ahead already. The agent grinned as he handed over a small memory stick to the Contact.

'It's a GIF,' he said tersely. 'The packet size is a bit large but that can't be helped. Once they play the GIF the patch merges into the circuitry. Only an analysis can detect it. Once implanted it has a lifespan of 30 days and then it just dies.' Mark continued, 'Just send it to your friend and have him send it to his sister, she can then send the GIF to the family and then we are on.'

The Contact nodded as he pocketed the memory stick. He was going to use a cheap disposable phone to send it to Idris with instructions to do the same while forwarding it to Zahi. The three men agreed to compare notes later and parted. The Contact walked to the metro deep in thought as he replayed the conversation in his mind.

Maldives

Ahmed Idris was in his office when the police arrived to seize his cell phone and laptop. There had been a small commotion in the reception area right outside his cabin and he had been about to use the intercom when the door opened outward and three officers of the Maldives police force walked in followed by his distraught receptionist. Simultaneously, the door opposite his cabin opened and the other staff peeked out in alarm. Despite his pounding heart Idris forced a convivial expression on his face and invited the policemen to take a seat. He instructed his receptionist to have some tea and water sent in, placing a hand on her shoulder in a reassuring gesture. After her departure Ahmed Idris closed the door and said lightly, 'Well, gentlemen, how may I be of service today?'

Senior Inspector Ishfaq, a round-shouldered bearded man replied, 'Mr Idris, I have here a court order authorizing me to seize your cell phones and personal laptop.' He pulled out a two-page document and handed it to Idris.

Idris sat at his desk and scanned the court order. It was obviously authentic and bore the familiar court seal. The order stated that the court having been satisfied that there was a strong possibility that Ahmed Idris possessed or was in the process of possessing and/or dessiminating information/material /documentation that had the capacity to jeopardize national security and create/sow discord among the public, and therefore it authorized the lawful seizure of his cell phone and laptop and subjection of the same articles to a forensic examination.

As he read the court order he sensed the three policemen shift impatiently in their chairs, and his stomach knotted into a cold ball of fury. Without a word he slid his cell phone towards Ishfaq and gestured with a flick of his wrist towards the laptop on his desk. Idris didn't trust himself to speak. He knew his childhood friend Muzzafar Salim had betrayed him. Suddenly, he was very much aware of the other cell phone, the one he used to contact Zahi and his friend. It was lying right next to the decorative vase connected to the charging port. A cursory glance at the other end of his office would reveal it. He had to get the policemen out of his office now. The officer wanted his signature on the receipt form and Idris complied briskly.

The officers weren't done yet. Senior Inspector Ishfaq produced another court order and placed it on the desk. 'This is a gag order from the court directing you not to disclose to any person or entity whether local or foreign about the seizure of all electronic devices taken from you for a period of three months from this date,' He added, 'I must inform you that at this moment a similar order is being served to your wife at your residence by my colleagues. Her cell phone and laptop have also been seized.'

Numbly Idris signed an acknowledgement to that effect and the three policemen finally filed out of his office. He followed them out into the reception area, a smile fixed unnaturally on his face, and then Ishfaq turned to the receptionist and waved Idris's phone at her. 'Does your boss have any other cell phone besides this one?' he asked, his eyes on the receptionist's face. Idris's stomach knotted again.

The receptionist looked squarely at the senior inspector's face, and then at the cell phone in his hand, a frown creased her forehead, and she slowly shook her head.

'No, that's the only phone Mr Idris carries,' she said.

The door closed behind the policemen, and Idris and the receptionist stood staring at one another.

United States

Half an hour later, the Contact was on the phone with the doctor. He had received a very agitated call from Ahmed Idris about the police raid and the seizures of the phones and laptops. While Idris's secret phone had escaped the police's attention, Dr Sameer's had been found on the living room table right next to his usual phone. Both Idris and the Contact knew that the police now had the Contact identified as a common factor. And the doctor's emails and texts would give them sufficient information to suspect that some kind of operation was being attempted. The Contact had immediately instructed Idris to dump his secret phone and SIM card and buy a new set. He would do the same and from now on, Idris was never to carry it on his person. He had to find a very safe place for it. Another police search and arrest couldn't be ruled out.

'So how are you holding up, Sameer?' he asked.

'It's difficult for us,' Sameer replied, 'people look at me as if I am a criminal. I am thinking of going somewhere abroad for further studies or work.'

The Contact nodded to himself. It must be indeed difficult for the doctor and his wife to deal with the unwelcome attention and scrutiny, to say nothing of the social ostracization that was bound to follow in certain segments of society.

'Has there been any contact from your siblings?' he queried. Now that the family had cell phones and Internet access there would be intermittent communication, however guarded. Most recruits and migrants to the Islamic State maintained secret communications with their parents, friends or other loved ones back home. Encrypted applications such as Telegram, Whatsapp, Trillion, Twitter and others were among the more popular. Other than exchanging messages of well-being these applications served as a vehicle for the Islamic State propaganda and as a tool for recruitment. The IS had also used these applications and their features as a weapon in the battlefield for calling in location details for precision strikes and for gathering real-time intelligence in shifting battlefield scenarios.

There was an almost imperceptible instant of hesitation before the doctor replied: 'No there is nothing, no news at all.'

The Contact took time digesting this unexpected response and then said, 'Well, let's hope they manage to get in touch soon enough. I am expecting some calls from my sources,too, so if there is any news at all I will get in touch with you.'

After the phone call the Contact continued sitting at his desk wondering why the good doctor had lied to him.

Maldives

Shaikh Adnan Shakil had just finished delivering a lecture to a batch of 30 young men, it was day 3 of a 7-day 'life skills' training course that his NGO regularly held all over the Maldives. The Shaikh was a tall, well-set man of forty with a luxuriant beard and a pair of soft but mesmeric brown eyes that held his listeners captive with an unwavering gaze. He was a man with the distinctive personal charisma that most born leaders possess. He returned to the room that served as a temporary office cum rest room for him. He gave instructions that he wasn't to be disturbed for the next hour and bolted the door from inside. His first call was to his old classmate and now policeman, Muzzafar Salim, which lasted twenty minutes with the Shaikh mostly listening and scribbling down notes. He asked the occasional question and noted the replies.

After the call Shaikh Adnan sat for a long time staring at the desktop, his upper teeth gnawing at his thick lower lip, an conscious mannerism he affected whenever he was ruminating on something that disturbed him. Idris's conversation and request to Salim about details of the Islamic State recruiters in Maldives, this—*mercenary*—in the United States of America, and the gist of all the details gleaned from Dr Sameer's cell phone and laptop, all pointed towards an effort to study the radicalization and recruitment process of the Islamic States machinery in the Maldives... to what end? And what about the pilot and his family, he had to be separated at once, that much was clear. An additional security layer had to be put in place immediately. It was not his responsibility but reporting an accurate assessment of the developments was. The Security Council in Syria was not going to be happy, this friend of Ahmed Idris's was a definite threat to the entire project and they would take the call on how to deal with him. As for Idris, he would have been sufficiently subdued by the police action and anyway Idris was too big and popular for the present, perhaps later one day....

Shaikh Adnan walked over to his shoulder-bag and removed a satellite phone, dialling a number from memory. After a series of clicks, the call went through and he started talking.

In his house at Nilandhoo. Dr Sameer Ibraheem was uncomfortable; lying wasn't part of his natural persona and the Contact was trying to help him. But now that his brothers and sisters had contacted him and he knew that they were deep inside Islamic State territory, what could anyone do? They were there voluntarily and it was impossible to convince them to return or for anyone to forcibly bring them back. They had cautioned him and he had started using an old cell phone that he kept hidden behind some jars of pickles in the pantry. The police had already confiscated his other phones and laptop and no doubt they would find the Contact's details there. So the doctor was reluctant to play any further part in the whole situation. There were no advantages or benefits for him now, only the risk of further alienation and the ire of the state agencies. Sameer walked outside his house and slowly wandered towards the beach; behind him his wife stood at the door of their house and followed him with her eyes.

CHAPTER FIFTEEN

Raqqa

The shadows shifted again as they did everytime he turned a corner, or passed under a bulb turning him into a shadow of an ogre sketched in black against the walls that seemed to move closer, more inward. A fine dust drifted down, its arrival heralded by a few grains of sand that dribbled with a scarcely discernable sound as some vehicles rumbled on the street overhead.

Abu Moumin al Fransisi, the chief of special operations (Europe & America) hunched lower as he navigated the maze of tunnels they had dug under Mosul. The thirty-six-year-old veteran of the Bosnian struggle had received Shaikh Adnan Shakil's call the night before, but security and operational exigencies dictated that he wait for dawn before using the tunnels to reach the other end of the town. The matter required a face-to-face briefing. The family was high-value, the pilot was special projects material, the women were young, there were the potential child soldiers, and two of the group had signed up for suicide missions at the time of registration. Overall, the family made for good publicity and the possibilities were beyond encouraging. He had made sure that the family had jumped the queue in terms of housing, and the ration cards had already been issued, which made the family privileged, which they recognized and appreciated. Doubtless they also recognized that there was a price to be paid.

The light grew brighter and the bulb became redundant as Moumin stepped into the basement of a house in the eastern sector and climbed up a flight of stairs. He stretched to ease his lower back and looked at his lieutenant for this sector, the gigantic and ever-smiling Abid Mossulman. He prepared himself for the inevitable—bone-crushing hug that followed. Allah! The man didn't know his own strength. The giant led Moumin into the house and a few minutes later the two men sat on cane chairs facing each other. Moumin had used the facilities to wash up and had tidied himself. He was taking the occasional sip of water from a glass and there were dates on the table. Abid listened avidly to his commander, interjecting only to verify a point or clarify an ambiguity.

'I want the pilot taken for photographs and documentation at the earliest. Make sure that someone is with him at all times. I don't want him exposed to any extra scrutiny so use the tunnels to the maximum,' Moumin instructed him. 'It will be unavoidable in some areas to surface and to use the streets, I know, but take care anyhow.'

Abid nodded to signify his understanding. Moumin resumed his instructions. 'Two of the family are on the volunteer martyrs' list, a husband-wife team, I believe. I want them transferred to Mosul next week,' he paused.

'They can serve the caliph better there.' Moumin looked directly at his lieutenant as he spoke.

Abid felt bigger somehow as he experienced the flush of being trusted with top-secret information. It was rumoured that the Leader was in Mosul, which was in danger of being encircled. The Leader had to get out of the city and a series of diversions were being arranged. Insha'Allah, no doubt both volunteers would play a part, may He continue to guide them.

'What arrangements are in place for keeping an eye on them?' Moumin queried.

'The Al Khaansa checks in on the women every couple of days, and but nothing apart from that at present. The men are awaiting deployment,' Abid clarifed.

'Well, tell the Al Khaansa to carry out daily checks from today onwards and have one of your men visit the house and look at their laptops and phones every week,' Moumin ordered.

After the lieutenant had left, Moumin took out his phone and opened one of his numerous Telegram accounts and tapped into the secret chat feature. He scrolled for and found the name he was looking for and then sent a text. A few moments later he received a reply. As per established security protocol, Moumin asked a predefined question: 'Salaam Valaikum, all well?'

The answer came: "Alhamdulillah, everything is well.'

Moumin smiled in satisfaction. The answer signified that the soldier at the other end was secure and not under duress, otherwise the answer would read: 'Alhamdulillah, all is well', in which case he would promptly close the account and dump the phone.

Over the few minutes Moumin gave the soldier all available details of the person who was helping Ahmed Idris, and then ordered his assassination by whatever means available.

United States

The soldier looked down at the screen and suddenly his palms were moist. This was it! An assignment at last, their first. The soldier was one of a group of three likeminded members of the IS and they called themselves the Jersey City Cell. He was ex-US army, and with his knowledge and training, the natural leader of the three. The other two were Aamir and Shahid. The former was a twenty-one-year-old college dropout with a history of drug abuse, since reformed, and now claimed to be a pious Muslim; Shahid was the scholarly one, the one with the degree in Middle Eastern studies, and helped his father run a convenience store.

The Jersey City Cell met twice a week in the soldier's garage and talked about the jihad. They had established communications with Abu Moumin Fransisi a year ago through one of the many chat rooms that the IS had convened and maintained in its recruitment and propaganda drive. These chat rooms frequently changed their name and application as a matter of routine. Identities were a closely guarded secret and often, one group was unaware of the existence of another even if they were in immediate geographical proximity. Moumin had inspired and cultivated them over the past year and now he reckoned they were ready for the test. If they succeeded and survived, they would be used for a bigger task, if not, there was no real harm done, and a clear message would be delivered regardless of the result.

Each member of the cell considered himself ready and capable to perform the ultimate sacrifice for the caliphate. They had all seen the footages of drone attacks, and the evils of idolatry, and non-Islamic religious beliefs that resulted in the marginalization of pure Islam that was happening all over the world. The Sharia had been corrupted and the very foundation of Islam was under threat, and they prayed everyday for an opportunity to serve and preserve it.

The soldier noted down the information given to him on a small piece of paper and saved the photograph on his device memory. He then deleted the entire chat from the application, as instructed by Abu Moumin. He would destroy the notes after they had been committed to memory. The soldier lost no time in texting the others; they would meet immediately at the garage.

Raqqa

The car stood outside the family's house, the driver scrubbing at its windshield with a damp cloth. He would alternate between using a damp and a dry rag until the plexiglass shone to his satisfaction. On their intended journey, mistaking a distant vehicle or aircraft for a speck of dust on the windshield could prove to be a fatal error, and the driver was a careful man.

Moisin Shameem, the Escort, and another man stood just outside the entrance of the house. Neither man looked at the other. Neither did they look or go inside, respecting the family's privacy especially at times such as these. Despite the scores of people he had travelled with over the last three years, the Escort remembered this family very well. He remembered picking them up at that border checkpoint at Kilis a few months earlier. Little did he think he would be seeing them again, so soon.

Inside the house the family had gathered in the living room at the request of Qassim and Zahara. They were all there except Aabir, who had been summoned by Abid Mossalman earlier that morning. It was quiet in the family living room, quiet except for the whispers and a stifled sob from the huddled women who held each other tightly, Zahi, too, among them. The men stood together, hands on each other's shoulders, Qassim looking at Munsiu with a gaze that was strangely peaceful. Indeed, Munsiu felt as though Qassim was looking through and beyond him.

The couple had called for everyone to assemble, and Zahara had smiled at them and simply said that they were leaving for another part of the country. Qassim stood by her side, his arm around her in what was for them a rare and open display of their love, and looked straight at Munsiu. After a moment of incomprehension, the other man's eyes had widened with understanding.

The women had barely begun with their bewildered queries when Zahara gently shushed them and explained that they wouldn't be coming back. It was what both of them wanted, she said in a calm voice, especially since she wasn't able to bear children. Zahara concluded by saying she and Qassim had discussed their decision at length, and now it was time to take it. The sobs had started when Zahara started dividing her jewellery, clothes and other knick-knacks and the women had reached out to each other in a tight group embrace, Zahara whispering into each one's ear, the smile never leaving her face. When she came to Zahi, she drew her sister-in-law close and murmured, 'Take care of my brother and give him sons.' Zahi couldn't speak and just stood looking at her, dimly aware of tears streaming down her cheeks.

Suddenly, it was time to go. The couple gently pushed the others away, the men hugged each other roughly one last time, and then they were gone, out of the house and into the waiting car, neither of them looking back again, and inside the house, the living room suddenly seemed very big and empty.

In the next couple of weeks Zahi noticed several alarming things. For one, the Al Khaansa came everyday, their eyes constantly probing, engaging them in conversations that were clearly intended to elicit an exact account of their activities on the preceding day. There was one amongst them, a tall, broad-shouldered woman with bony features, who looked at Zahi with something akin to hunger in her eyes. She seemed to take every opportunity to touch Zahi and stood too close when she talked. Zahi hated her.

The security patrol had come twice and examined their phones and the laptops. That had never happened before. Ahmed Idris had told Zahi about the police raid at his office and residence, and had instructed her to be very, very careful. They no longer communicated daily and sometimes it was three or four days before she used the phone to check for messages or send any. She had received the Spore software from Idris and had forwarded it to the family chat group from the new cell phone device that Munsiu had brought for her. She didn't understand fully why her brother had asked her to do that, but she knew that it had to be important. The phone used to communicate with her brother was now no longer in their room, but lay switched off behind a loose brick in the courtyard compound wall to the rear of the house. It was the only place that wasn't visible from any window or door and she took it out only at night for a few risky minutes, and then back it went into the niche. It was getting increasingly dangerous now to use it.

Zahi looked across the courtyard at Aabir playing with Haifa, his niece, and she smiled involuntarily. The young man had been inconsolable on his return that day, to find his sister and Qassim gone. Abbu had retreated to his room and hadn't come out for days. Zahi had asked him where he had been, and he had been uncharacteristically reticent about the whole thing. She didn't press him after that.

Aabir looked up and his eyes met Zahi's. The young man smiled at her, a quick flash of bright white teeth with the corners of his eyes crinkling, and she smiled back. Of the entire family he was her favourite, and to her, the biggest surprise. He was the last person she expected to embark on such a misadventure, but then, Zahi thought, how little do I know about human nature. She had failed to read her own husband's mind. Now, she was learning, and learning fast.

Aabir turned his attention back to Haifa. He thought back to the day he had returned to find Zahara and Qassim gone. He wouldn't see them again, he knew. He had gone with the huge Adil Mossalman to the administrative office of the Wilaayat, and they had taken his photograph, several times, and in two sets of clothes. An hour's wait, and then he had been handed a pass that would take him past most checkpoints. The pass was valid for a month. No explanations had been forthcoming about the pass and he had learnt enough not to ask questions. Abid had instructed him to keep a suitcase packed ready to go at an instant's notice. He was also asked to purchase and keep a brand new phone and stash it in the suitcase unused. The suitcase was not to contain any article that would indicate a presence in Syria or the Middle East. The giant had handed him several articles of branded clothing, all in their original packing. A set of Gillette toiletries and shaving gear completed the ensemble; the underwear was, likewise, of a popular Western brand.

United States

The Contact had just got back on to the deck, after having fed the koi watching and admiring the kaleidoscopic patterns their colours formed with each swift, gliding movement. He was filling up the dog's food bowl when the phone rang. He allowed it to ring while he topped up the water bowl and, after giving the animal a few pats, he walked over to check who had called. He frowned as he saw Captain Brar's number; he wasn't expecting any calls from the mariner. The Contact dialled back, and a moment later was deep in conversation with the Captain. The conversation lasted a long time, during which he took copious notes. The call ended with an agreement to have another update two days hence. The Contact then swiftly dialled another number, this time in Oman. After a few rings, Dilawar Choudhary came on the line and the two men spoke to each other in quick, urgent tones. Across the room, the dog sensed the tension, stopped eating and looked up, keeping his eyes fixed unwaveringly on the Contact.

CHAPTER SIXTEEN

The entire frame juddered as the brakes came on and the plane rapidly lost ground speed, the sound of the engine revs suddenly very loud like a roar. The tires hissed on the runway, the noise dying as swiftly as it reached taxiing speed. It had been a soft landing, and the runway was still smooth despite the increased aircraft traffic these last two decades. The French built good airports. The passengers rocked to a halt in the parking bay and were already standing impatiently in the aisle by the time the airbridge connected. Dilawar Choudhary preferred to sit. He would be amongst the last to deplane; he never understood this haste to disembark. After all, they would all have to wait at the baggage concourse. The baggage delivery was notoriously tardy at the Baghdad International Airport.

The spice trader and part-time smuggler had dispatched his son Yasser ahead of him a week earlier, as soon as he had got off the phone with the Contact. The young man was waiting for him just outside the arrivals gate of Terminal 3, and hurried forward to take the suitcase from his father's hand. They walked to the uncovered car park, and got into a Mitsubishi Outlander that Yasser had rented. Dilawar sighed in pleasure as the air conditioner kicked in. Damn! He was getting soft and used to the luxuries, he thought.

On cold wintry mornings, it took five minutes to get out of bed these days. He wondered if the Contact faced the same reality of age and shook his head. You never knew with that one; he was seemingly indestructible.

The spice trader's memory relived that time in the Baluchistan sector when he had been holed up in a mud hut and down to his last two magazine loads. By Allah, he had thought then, it's my time and there is no seed to carry my name forward. Dilawar had hugged the ground closer as the bullets punched through the earth and rough bricks in a pattern obviously designed to cover every inch of the failing structure he was trapped within. Soon, they would start with the RPGs, which were indefensible, and death seemed inevitable, so he had decided to take as many he could with him, in one wild last charge across the fifty-yard clearing. The Contact had then miraculously appeared like a ghost, taking the man on the right who had Dilawar pinned down with a M26 grenade, and then raking the other end with an accurate burst of the Heckler & Koch that lasted a full five seconds. Afterwards Dilawar, had nearly puked his guts out before he dared taste the possibility of life once more. He had, however, taken a 7.62 mm round in the calf and the Contact had to half carry him the five miles to safety, before plugging both entry and exit holes and depositing him on a truck to the airfield. The wound had throbbed agonizingly, and the memory caused his leg to twitch violently even now, against the floorboards of the Mitsubishi. Yasser glanced at his father and recognized the expression. He had seen it before and said nothing now. There are things a man prefers not to talk about, and those boundaries are to be respected. Father and son completed the ten-mile journey to the small flat they maintained in the city in silence, with the spice trader checking his phone every now and then for texts and emails.

At the flat they got right down to business. The operational schedule had been advanced and there was a lot to be done. Yasser had been busy acquiring transit passes for any excursion into Islamic State territory in both Syria and Iraq. It helped that father and son were major buyers of scrap and equally dependable suppliers of grain, spices and electronics, having the Turkey-Manhbij, Aleppo, Raqqa and Homs route in Syria pretty much covered. They had similar trade acquaintances in the Mosul, Irbil and Kirkuk sector. The plan they had devised depended on flexibility and the ability to travel in more directions than one. They knew dozens of traders that did business in the area; there was a flourishing commerce in medical supplies, uniforms, toiletries, dried and canned foods, in short, everything that a country would need, for the Islamic State was a country, and its exports were oil, agricultural produce, kidnap and ransom, refugee transportation and ideology. Passes for trade and business, that authorized transport of men and materials, were routinely issued, and, as is the practice the world over, such passes often became currency or bargaining chips. The validity and nature of the passes dictated their value.

They discussed and finalized the vehicles to be used, everything had to be well maintained and dependable—yet not too new or flashy. The idea was to not deviate from the norm. Weapons were discussed, and bodyguards. The last was special, and so they chose trust over efficiency. They settled upon a mix of old-timers and some of Yasser's lot, young, fearless and fanatically loyal. Dilawar deferred to his son on this.

Yasser's phone chirped. He picked it up and spoke into it, smiling. After a minute he turned to his father and said

'They are here, the kids too.'

Dilawar's features creased into a similar smile. 'Give me the phone,' he said.

Maldives

Ahmed Idris was on the phone with his friend and he couldn't choose between exhilaration and unadulterated anxiety. 'How can that be arranged so soon?' he asked. 'Do you think—'

'No other option now, Ahmed,' the Contact interjected. 'She has to be ready.' The contact paused and asked, 'What's your read on her?'

Idris didn't hesitate for a moment, he knew his sister. Ever since she had been a toddler, she had been loving and ready to share her stuff, whether it was a toy or a treat, and these traits had carried over into the making of a lovely young woman. She had done well in college and had not demurred when a husband had been chosen for her and accorded her in-laws and new relatives the same affection and respect she gave her own. Like everyone else, her new family found her to be polite, caring and cooperative, which she was. What they didn't know was that the young bride was also a strong-willed woman who had a spirited streak in her. When denied something Zahi would never throw a tantrum or sulk, she would instead proceed to determine how to get what she wanted, and usually succeeded. He had seen it happen many a time before.

'My sister will do whatever has to be done, I am positive about that.' Idris's voice carried conviction, and at the other end, the Contact nodded.

'Good, now remember, tell her that from the time it's a go, she has to be ready to make the rendezvous. It could be any of the next three nights,' the Contact said crisply. 'Make that absolutely clear to her. She *cannot* not turn up. Our man won't be able to make a second run.'

'I understand, my friend. I'll make sure she understands, too,' Idris replied.

'And you, my friend, have to be extra careful these next few weeks,' the Contact instructed further. 'Don't lose that temper of yours and don't create any waves. Let it be business as usual, and take especial care of the phone. We can't afford to have you arrested at this stage.'

'And what about you?' queried Ahmed Idris. 'Because of that bastard Muzzafar your identity is exposed now.'

'Oh, I wouldn't worry about that,' the Contact replied lightly. 'I can take care of myself, and besides, if you consider it from a holistic point of view, I am not that important in the scheme of things anyway.'

United States

The Jersey City Cell had the Contact under watch; it was necessarily a very loose form of surveillance, depending upon the times and duration of their availability, and hence quite haphazard, and it was precisely because of that that the Contact didn't spot them. Sometimes, one or two of them would park their car several houses up or down from the Contact's residence but never for long. It was a quiet neighbourhood, and two men parked in an unknown car would soon attract attention, so they adapted and used other tactics. There was a small coffee shop on the main street and from there they could keep a watch for the Contact or his car and take it from there. The cell put in two, sometimes three, hours of this slack surveillance daily. The soldier had conducted a reconnaissance of the immediate area around the house and they had found a small strip of parking space in the lane behind from where they could see part of the backyard, but that was about it. They couldn't see the front door and hence had no line of sight of his coming or going. Besides, they had seen the dog and that had cancelled any sort of stealthy infiltration into his house. Also, as the soldier observed, they had no clue about the interiors apart from the sketchy details they had acquired from perusing the house's earlier listing on the real estate websites.

The man they watched had no discernable pattern to his daily routine; he didn't go to an office so his movements were dictated apparently by convenience and whim. He went to the local supermarket, the library, the convenience store, New York City and the park. He always went to the park accompanied by the large wolf-like dog in the back of the car, and sometimes walking the half-mile there along Gilford Drive before covering the last couple of hundred yards on Primrose Avenue to enter the park. The Contact went to the park every day and sometimes twice, and it was increasingly evident that the park was the most predictable movement in the Contact's otherwise erratic itinerary.

So the members of the Jersey City Cell watched and talked, and they discussed their resources and the various options available to kill the Contact.

Raqqa, Eastern Sector

Abu Momim al Fransisi was deep in conversation with his counterpart Sayyed Mujahid, a fierce-looking Afghan from the Kandahar region of Afghanistan. Sayyed, a tall lean man, whose already forbidding appearance was accentuated by the fact that he was missing half a left ear supervised the recruitment and formation of cells in the Asian (India-Bangladesh-

Sri Lanka-Maldives) theatre. Sayyed was describing the composition of the cells to Momin who found it fascinating, more so since the old Afghan warrior had been so phenomenally successful in his efforts. At the time, there were 25 cells in that theatre, most unaware of the others' existence.

'You see, my brother,' the old warrior was saying, 'we primarily look for youth who have stayed at and received tuition at the madarsas, because only such schools teach the true meaning of our faith, not the watered-down version that these soft-bellied pseudo mullahs peddle in the name of Islam. Further, we look for a balanced composition of uneducated youth with some mechanical aptitude, and those with a degree or experience in computers or chemical engineering. It's been my experience that the sons of scholars, butchers and scrap-dealers make for good candidates.'

Sayyed hawked and Momin tried not to wince as his brother-in-arms expertly spat out a thick gob of phlegm. It landed with a muted splat some feet away. Both men were sitting under a Lebanese cedar with their bodyguards maintaining a fifty-yard distance. Momin had received confirmation about the couple's arrival in Mosul and had activated the movement order of the pilot. Everything was on schedule as far as the family was concerned.

'Once we have five or six soldiers which, as you know, is the preferred number of recruits to form a basic cell, we instruct them to have a meeting which is controlled by whom we judge to be the natural leader of the bunch. But before that we find out who has the means to reach the caliphate without our financial assistance, and if there are cases where there is a sponsor, then we take those on a case-to-case basis.' Sayyed Mujahid paused and looked around, taking his time to study the surroundings. After a while, he went on, 'At the meeting the group is initiated by oath and become sworn soldiers of what we call 'Jundul Caliphate-beHind' which we have declared as supportive to the Islamic State, the psychology being that the members understand that they are still under examination and not fully accepted yet.

'In this meeting a working set-up is created by votes, and the structure is as followed on a national level, as well as the state. There are to be four basic departments and these would be developed based on progress made. These are dawati (recruitment), maali (finance), askari (defence) and media (information).' Sayyed spat by way of punctuation.

'This appointment of officials always creates a sense of purpose in any group. Remember, my brother, if there is no purpose and no leadership, then all gatherings are but a herd of mindless sheep waiting for the knife, but once there is discipline and a plan added to the mix... then we have a working cell,' he concluded.

The two men shifted focus and discussed operational tactics for the next hour, before the food arrived. It was simple but delicious fare: minced meat kibbeh with freshly baked manoushi bread and the tart Syrian hummus. The meal ended with the inevitable cup of coffee and syrupy baklava on the side, and soon thereafter, sated, they departed to their respective commands.

On his way back, Abu Momin al Fransisi considered what he had just heard. How true, he reminisced, and how simple. Give a group a source of danger, arm them with ideals and point them towards a target, and lo and behold, we have ourselves a working and motivated cell. They reached the residential quadrant and one by one, each man bent forward to pass through the low doorway that led to the tunnels. On his return to his headquarters, Momin gave orders to the Jersey City Cell to expedite matters with urgency.

United States

Mark Ross studied the call detail records with a mixture of pride and alarm. This morning, he had two analysts reporting to him for temporary duty, and it either meant that the intel coming in was budget-worthy or else he was being set up for the chop. Mark was confident that it was the former and he considered sharing part of the findings with the Contact. The man was obviously well connected and could add value to the analysis by having the Zahi girl play a bigger role—but that was a call for his boss to take. From what Mark could see they had 'an in' to at least half a dozen numbers and those had already been tagged for the watchlist. In the algorithms that would come into play as a matter of course, each of these highlighted numbers had the potential to reveal intelligence that could prove crucial.

The FBI agent wondered if he should call the Contact for a meet, and then decided to hold off for a bit. Besides, he had that money-laundering investigation going on, and had to work on that too. Mark Ross sighed and reached for the phone. He was going to be late again tonight. He'd better tell his wife. He wasn't looking forward to this conversation. It was the third time he had cancelled this month.

CHAPTER SEVENTEEN

Mosul

The thing looked like something out of a *Mad Max* movie in the cold morning light, a beast bedecked with diamonds of dew, some of which had just begun to streak down its iron flanks in shiny rivulets. Qassim examined the armoured sides with the fascination of one who knows that his flesh would have melded for an eternity with the beast's metals before the sun had set today. Over the last few days, he had become intimately familiar with the machine, the engineer in him appreciating the inventiveness of the designers who had built it.

The Islamic State's swift takeover of vast territories in Iraq and Syria resulted in the capture of large numbers of military vehicles and equipment such as tanks, armoured personnel carriers, other armoured vehicles, artillery pieces, ammunition, as well as several types of heavy and light military gear. These acquisitions had dramatically altered the battlefield conditions. The Islamic State army seized approximately 2,300 US-manufactured Humvees (high-mobility multipurpose wheeled vehicles) in the city of Mosul alone. In addition there were captured civilian vehicles, commercial trucks, buses, bulldozers, dump trucks and a host of other vehicles. And so started the industry of building the VBIED or vehicle-borne improvised explosive device. It could be driven and left in close proximity of a target to be detonated remotely, or by a timed fuse.

The newest VBIED iteration represented a significant improvement on the earlier models, in that the mobile bomb was now not only mobile, but also *armoured*, and that vastly increased its survival probability of reaching the intended target. These armoured suicide bombing vehicles were now utilized either individually or in groups against secure compounds and high-value infrastructure and were far less vulnerable to defending fire than the earlier unarmoured variant.

The Islamic State's use of VBIEDs had now evolved to the point where they had been used even *en masse*, with 30 huge mobile bombs deployed simultaneously during the capture of the Iraqi city of Ramadi in May 2015. Qassim had listened with rapt attention as the brigade commander had narrated how, in the first wave, the attacking squadron had first sent in a bulldozer packed with explosives which had successfully obliterated a security perimeter around an Iraqi government compound. Immediately after, a convoy of about 30 vehicles flooded into the then contested city, setting off another series of massive explosions. The Islamic State's hordes had followed that up by descending in a wild-eyed screaming mass upon the paralyzed defence and taken the city.

Qassim had even learnt to his amazement that there was another variant in the planning, The workshops in the Nineveh plains areas had been experimenting, and had almost perfected several prototypes of a driverless vehicle. This meant that a suicide driver would no longer be required to drive the vehicle bomb into its intended target. Instead, a remote-controlled steering, accelerating and braking system would do the job. This variant also included a mannequin rigged with thermal-output capability to mimic the heat signature given off by a human driver. This was to fool any use of thermal-sensing equipment at secure-facility access points, and road security checkpoints, and to make it register as if a human being was driving the vehicle.

The beast that Qassim would drive had been packed with 500 pounds of military-grade explosive and 300 pounds of homemade explosives. It also carried 200 pounds of shrapnel in the form of scrap metal. It had originally been a medium-size dumpster and now was covered with both sloped and slat armor.

Qassim's beast was equipped with plates of 100 mm thick armour sloped at 45 degrees at the front, and this effectively gave him 141 mm of armour. The intent was to increase the effective thickness for frontal impacts such as incoming fire by assault rifles and machine guns. With a bit of luck this was also sufficient to deflect or stop even anti-tank ammunition because, when a projectile hits sloped armour, its path might curve, forcing it to move through more armour or bounce off entirely.

The beast also boasted slat armour in the form of a metal grid of steel bars fitted over the improvised armour-plating with a space of about 8 inches between them. This provided an increased stand-off distance between any explosion or projectile impact and the vehicle, thereby reducing the projectile's penetration capabilities. The intention was to keep Qassim alive until he reached the target and also to protect the payload from premature detonation.

Qassim had bathed an hour before and the others had gathered around him before leaving. Most of them communicated the depth of their emotions with a rough masculine embrace, or a shaking of hands accompanied by a nod. Zahara had already left, and he tried to close his mind to all thoughts of her. They had spent their last day together and wouldn't see each other again. Their time together had been soft, it had been sweet, and it had given him unimaginable joy. But that was then, and now he had his task ahead of him—as she had hers.

Qassim pulled at the door on the driver's side. It was extremely heavy and came open slowly since it had been loaded with shrapnel placed in crude metal tubes that had been bracketed to the inner side. The detonation mechanism was fitted on the panel beside the steering wheel, and consisted of two sets of safeties and firing switches. Each set of safety and firing switches was connected to a separate firing circuit—for an obvious reason. The second set of buttons acted as a fail-safe in case the wiring on the first set turned out to be faulty or was damaged.

The beast growled to life at the turn of the ignition, and Qassim engaged gear. He didn't look outside at the others, the time for that had passed. The memory foam of the ear set nestled snugly in his ears and the plugged-in cord snaked down the sides of his neck to his breast pocket, where the phone was secured. All he had to do was reach into the pocket to receive a call. Qassim applied more pressure on the gas pedal and the beast moved forward slowly because of the weight of the armour and the payload. He would have to compensate for that, he thought, as he negotiated the doors of the workshop and proceeded towards the standby area with a deep rumbling sound that vibrated his seat.

The standby area was behind a row of single-storey shops that bordered a two-lane road that went half a mile south before joining an intersection that led out of the city. The intersection was manned by two checkposts and a mobile attack/defence unit of one M1A1 Abrams tank and two M113 armoured personnel carriers. Qassim switched off the engine and pushed the door slightly open to allow some air in. He looked at the twin set of firing switches again, and wondered for the hundredth time if he would feel anything in the instant of explosion. Some burning or some beginning of pain in the infinitesimal fraction of a second before he vaporized? Probably not, he decided, and anyway it was now not a moot point. He would do what he had to regardless. It was for Islam, and he would get his 'Sawab', his reward. Time trickled by and Qassim waited....

Zahara thought lovingly of her husband all the time. Four miles east, she walked at a steady unhurried pace on the pavements of the marketplace. The vest they had strapped on her torso wasn't very heavy—about 15 pounds or so—but it chafed at the shoulders and a dull ache had begun to form just below the back of her neck. She recognized it as tension as her back muscles compensated for the unfamiliar weight and the sweat caused her robe to stick to her body. The body bomb was a simple-enough device with the power supplied by a flat battery pack and a basic flip switch. The other, smaller, charge was in the shopping bag she carried and the trigger switch was sewn on the handle just an inch and a half away from her thumb. Each device was independent of the other and both were to be detonated at the same time. That way, even if one switch were to malfunction, the explosion of the other charge would result in sympathetic detonation of the failed bomb. Eyes fixed ahead on the target, Zahara walked on, a strange calm settling over her. Soon, she told herself, soon….

The phone rang in his ears and he reached for it, the other hand slamming shut the door. The voice spoke in an unhurried and calm tone, making sure that he understood the instructions, and Qassim started his metal beast, revving it slightly before putting it in gear. He edged around the line of shops and looked at the checkposts ahead of him, as he watched a Humvee approach the intersection from the far side, careening over the flat hard road. A few seconds later, the tank turret swivelled towards it. The two brown and green camouflaged M113s started speeding towards the Humvee which now had begun a series of zigzags dodging incoming fire and a 20-foot-tall eruption of sand, and signposted a near miss from the tank. This was the diversion and as every eye watched the Humvee hurtle towards the intersection, Qassim floored the pedal, his beast picking up speed rapidly to cover the half mile, *the half mile*—'Allah, be merciful,' prayed Qassim as he willed the huge metal beast to go faster. The beast vibrated and bounced as it sped onwards and the extra weight threatened to pull it off the road. Qassim fought the steering wheel to keep the beast on course as he peered through the narrow grill. He was now a bare 400 yards away and the beast howled as if in anticipation as it gained even more speed.

The Humvee had stopped by now about 300 yards from the checkpoint crippled beyond repair, and the soldier inside flipped on the toggle that detonated 200 pounds of explosive charge. Qassim didn't even hear the explosion and the blast wave didn't reach him inside the cabin. A mere 150 yards to go, and the tank barrel pointed at him now, the gunner desperately trying to lower elevation, and the rain of light-assault weapons' ammunition peppered the front armour of the beast ineffectually. There was no thought in his mind as his pupils dilated and with a hoarse incoherent atavistic yell, Qassim's fingers raised the plastic protective cap and flicked the firing switch. The beast disappeared in orange and black upwards and outwards a dozen yards from the intersection and when the smoke and dust had cleared, nothing remained alive but the thunder of the explosion that seemed to last an eternity.

Zahara heard the twin explosions rolling overhead. The second one was much more powerful and she instinctively looked upward and back as did most of the people on the street. She turned forward to the woman ahead of her—Zahara didn't even know her name, there was no need to—was now just a couple of dozen paces away from the gate with the guards and the jeeps with mounted machineguns. The woman made a quick sharp signal and Zahara turned to her left to duck into a grocer's store and waited for the explosion. It came a minute later as the woman detonated her vest, taking with her the guards and the jeeps and part of the gates in an instant fireball. The pieces of debris were still raining down on the rooftops, and the wounded had just begun screaming when Zahara walked through the gates and started running towards the ammunition dump, her left hand reaching inside the slit of her robe and feeling for the switch. The sentry at the dump was a young boy of nineteen and his hands shook as he nudged the selection lever to rapid fire, and Zahara spun to her right as the first round hit her in the right shoulder, the shopping bag falling from her suddenly nerveless fingers, and she crumpled on top of it. The shock of the 7.62 mm round numbed her for a few long seconds and as the pain started coming in waves, the sentry kept firing. She was on her back now and through a haze she saw the sky above. With an effort her left hand moved over the vest and found the switch, and in the instant before the explosion, she thought of her husband again. The blast killed no one else but her leaving behind just a few lumps of charred flesh, the rest of her body had simply vaporized and there was no damage, just a small smoking crater on the ground.

Raqqa

Zahi placed the glass of water on the table where Munsiu could easily reach it. Her husband looked up from the laptop and nodded. It wasn't an appreciative nod, more like an official acknowledging a lowly functionary performing a paid task. The nods made her want to pick up something heavy and bring it down with all her strength on his head repeatedly. Munsiu had been appointed to the office of supply chain logistics, and evidently reveled in his duties. The appointment had also made him insufferable and he spent long hours after work sitting on the corner table in their room pouring over names, numbers and other details that, according to him, were incalculably vital to the caliphate. Zahi had reported this to her brother and on his instructions she used a memory stick and downloaded his work folder every week. It was safe since he brought the laptop home every evening and they both used it. It was a matter of a couple of minutes and she generally did it when he went to the upper floor to chat with his sisters. She bolted the door from inside to prevent him from entering suddenly and catching her in the act. Zahi had once looked at a few files of the folder and to her they mainly consisted of spreadsheets involving bank accounts, fund transfers and invoice details. But she knew the folder contained vital details about the Islamic State's business identities all over the globe.

Munsiu had spoken to her about the importance of his position. The caliphate depended upon a host of exports and imports to survive as a country and there were several labyrinths of shell companies and financial institutions that ensured that it did. He had the responsibility of updating the daily records and did so with an assiduousness that bordered on the obsessive. So Zahi listened to his daily monologues patiently, looking into his eyes with an engaging smile on her face, and she waited for her brother's friend to come and take her out of this place.

CHAPTER EIGHTEEN

The plan to kill the Contact was a good one and very likely to succeed. It had the advantage of being simple and a proven efficacy over the last 100-plus years. The Jersey City Cell of the Islamic State had decided upon the 'drive by shooting' option to eliminate their target. The requirements were minimal: a weapon, a getaway vehicle and a place of their choosing that afforded a quick exit. And they had all three.

The soldier knew his weapons and had chosen the Colt AR-15 assault rifle, a weapon that was illegal in the state of New Jersey and fires .223 caliber ammunition. The magazine is built to accommodate a maximum of 10 rounds, each of which contains 77 grains of powder that provide 1300 pounds per square foot of impact energy to the bullet. The rifle weighed just 8 lbs unloaded, which made it lighter than most other rifles, and with an overall length of 39 inches, it was relatively small. Which is what made it more suitable for handling in the cramped confines of a car. They had decided to keep all the windows open to dissipate the sound. The soldier had acquired the rifle a few years ago, and he did not have any papers for it. Hence, it could be safely disposed of, after wiping it free of prints.

The car was a black 2013 Nissan Altima, with a 3.5 litre-engine; it had a lot of miles on it but was in decent shape, and anyhow, if it came to a police pursuit situation, the game was up anyway. The car was adequate for the operation, and they had stolen it earlier in the day. It now carried fake registration plates and was indistinguishable from a thousand others like it on the roads.

They were in the first parking lot, waiting for a call from Shahid who would give them the heads-up as soon as the Contact reached Primrose Avenue. They had picked the spot carefully. The road was bordered on one side by backyard fences of the houses there, and on the other by a high steel mesh fence separating the road from the state railway tracks. The target would have no place to hide and nowhere to run. The soldier wiped his palms on his jeans and tried to relax. Despite his service he had never been in combat before and he was nervous, he knew, confident, but nervous all the same. The rifle lay on the floor of the car and he glanced down at it every few moments. Aamir carried a Smith & Wesson 9 mm, tucked into the waistband of his pants under his shirt, just in case. Both men kept a watch for any cruising police patrols.

Aamir, the college dropout, was the driver and he mentally rehearsed his role. He was to proceed at a steady speed of 40 miles per hour and come to a stop about 20 yards away from the target. The Contact would be walking towards them and that was unavoidable, as there was no parking on Primrose and hence they had to park ahead. After the shooting, Aamir had to accelerate up the road that reached the parkway a mere mile ahead, where they would blend with the evening traffic. A dozen miles more would bring them to forest land, where they would wipe the inside of the car with a rag and some bleach and torch it before getting into Rashid's car and heading back to the garage. Both men waited for the phone to ring, and the tension in the car rose with every minute.

New York

Mark Ross stared at his section chief in puzzlement and said, 'Chief, we can really milk this. I mean there is fresh data coming in everyday.'

The section chief threw up his palms, clearly as frustrated as his agent. 'I know, Mark,' he said, the irritation evident in his voice, 'how do you think I feel?, A potential treasure trove of intel, but the powers that be have spoken.' The section chief paused and added, pragmatically, 'with a US-trained pilot out there, it's too big a risk, and they want this wrapped up asap.'

Mark looked at his boss. He knew what the man meant by 'wrapped up', and his first thought was about how the Contact would react. He wasn't looking forward to that conversation. Or perhaps the man didn't need to know. The FBI Agent looked up at the chief again and asked, 'When?'

The section chief considered the question for a long moment, his eyes locked with Mark's, replied, 'I'll let you know when.'

Which, Mark ruminated on the way back to his desk, was as cryptic an answer as any. His mind went back to the Contact and he wondered what the man was doing.

***

The car braked too hard, too late, and the Contact recognized the profile of the AR-15 as the man in the rear seat was jolted forward and the Nissan came to a complete stop 15 feet away. By that time the Contact was already running towards the car.

In 1983, a Sergeant Dennis Tueller of Salt Lake, Utah, conducted an experiment on how quickly a running man with a knife could cover a distance of 21 feet. The result was an average of 1.5 seconds. The Contact's limbs had limbered up by the half-mile walk and he had already been in motion, and so inertia wasn't a factor, and he beat the Tueller average angling left and nearer to the car and reaching it just as the muzzle of the AR-15 emerged out of the window. His left hand clawed the driver's face and raked downwards while his right grabbed the muzzle just as the soldier reflexively pulled the trigger. The bullet travelled skywards and the Contact started screaming to provide sound shock. He jerked the rifle downwards, maintaining that vector, because the shooter couldn't exert any appreciable pull at that angle and started losing grip of his weapon. Again, the left-handed clawing action this time, following it up with a punch to the driver's face and drawing blood as the lips were crushed against teeth. The Contact never stopping the screaming and the yanking on the rifle. The dog had by now overcome its astonishment and lunged at the rear window, almost clambering inside, and the soldier yanked himself away. The driver reached for his Smith & Wesson, his eyes watering but his head jerked sideways as the Contact grabbed his hair and twisted, the AR-15 now clattering on the road. The Contact kicked it under the Nissan before turning and vaulting over the fence and racing through the row of perennials and leaping over to the other side until he reached the lane beyond, the big dog following him and the Contact reaching for his cell phone to dial 911. By the time the cruiser arrived, he had a poop bag over his left hand.

The soldier leapt out of the black Nissan, cursing in a low monotone, and hooked out the rifle from under the car, Seconds later they were racing towards the parkway the soldier berating his companion all the way.

Raqqa

Zahi and Munsiu crossed the street after exiting the park behind them. Zoona and Lena followed a few paces behind with the children, and the family made their way through the street that led to their house. Aabir had gone to the administration office in the afternoon and hadn't returned yet. Zahi had noticed that for the last few days Abbu seemed to be constantly at the office and rarely returned home in time to have dinner with them. Lena always waited till his return and the siblings would eat together. It had always been that way. The street grew darker as they walked, there was a power cut again, and these had increased in their frequency. Some evenings they had just two hours of electricity. Lena and Zoona had started working, Lena at the primary school, and Zoona at the city supermarket, in the packaging division with the other women. Zahi herself had been reluctant to work in this place and, to her relief, Munsiu declared that there was no need for her to work.

Zahi had also noticed that in Raqqa, the state surveillance had been ramped up. Now there were cameras on major roads and near the Islamic State headquarters, to keep a close eye on the civilians, and the patrols of the local police were unrelenting in their random searches. The Hisbah grew stricter every day; only last week, a woman had been penalized for listening to music on her cell phone. Music was declared to be 'haraam', and the penalty for listening to or playing it was 25 lashes. Zahi had casually examined the primary textbooks and had been horrified to see the illustrations for a alphabet textbook depicting bullets, bombs, rockets and tanks—in short all things military and violent—and examination questions for a seven-year-old comprised essays on 'My Father as a Suicide Bomber' and 'My First Beheading of a Kaffir'. So, as the family reached their home, and Munsiu opened the gates, Zahi realized that in Raqqa, this was the new normal.

United States

Lieutenant Dave Eggleston of the New Jersey State Police moved his considerable bulk in his chair and peered out at the man sitting in the waiting room once again. The man appeared calm and was looking at the activity in the police station with evident interest. Eggleston turned back to Trooper Manfred (Manny) Delgado and asked, 'What the hell is that on his hand?'

Manny Delgado was two years old in the state police and had begun to think he had seen it all. This was a new education, and he shifted uneasily and replied, 'He says it's to preserve DNA sir, wouldn't let me see, just gave me this number and said, "Call that."' Manny shifted again and continued, 'I did call, sir. An FBI type answered, some Mark Ross, and he said they are on their way over here now. I asked the guy some questions (the trooper motioned with his head towards the Contact) but he said the Feds would explain everything.'

Trooper Manfred Delgado cleared his throat and continued to his best, 'He doesn't seem to have any injuries and, oh yes, he has a dog, sir.'

'What?' The lieutenant's bushy eyebrows joined together to support the furrows that creased his forehead.

'Him, sir, he had a dog with him, a big nasty one too, it's in the cruiser, Sir'. The trooper summoned up his young courage once more and said, 'Shall I go, sir?'

'What?' Eggleston snapped. 'Yeah, okay, you get back to your route—and let's have no loose chat on this,' he cautioned the trooper who turned to go and then stopped in his tracks, 'What about the dog, sir?'

'What?' The lieutenant barked again.

'The dog, sir,' a visibly discomfited Manny Delgado repeated. 'Shall I bring it to him? Or shall I call animal control?'

The lieutenant thought for a moment. The man was apparently a victim, the dog hadn't hurt anyone and the Fed's were due any minute in connection with this whole affair.

'Oh, for Christ's sake, just take the man out to the cruiser and let him bring it in. Tell him to come to my cabin.' Trooper Delgado hurried out and Dave Eggleston settled back in his chair and waited. Five minutes later the Contact entered the cabin holding the door open wide to allow the dog to come in. The animal sniffed around a few moments and then curled up against the door while the police officer examined the man across the table. Like most good officers, the lieutenant was a swift and good judge of people, and so he stood up and extended his hand, saying, 'Right, can you tell me exactly what's going on, sir?'

An hour later the Contact was in an agency car with Mark Ross. The poop bag and the Contact's hand had been swabbed for DNA sampling, and alternative lodgings for the Contact had to be found.

Raqqa

Aabir sat in the darkened room in the personal chambers of Abu Momin Al Fransisi, and he couldn't stop weeping. The giant Abid Mossulman watched him but offered no comfort. The youth had to learn that he didn't have the luxury of having a shoulder to cry on, and he had to believe that every act was justified by the Koran when it was done in furtherance of Islam. They had just shown Aabir a videotape of his sister Zahara and his brother-in-law Qassim. The couple had spoken to Abbu from beyond their nonexistent graves and extorted him to continue the jihad. They had told him that they were waiting. The tape had lasted five minutes and they had closely watched the young man's face as it traversed expressions from shock to grief to anger and finally, the cold deadly rage that they had sought to inspire. Both men looked at each other and smiled in satisfaction.

CHAPTER NINETEEN

Zahi was alone in the house when the text arrived. The women had gone to work, the children were in the daycare, and Munsiu had just left for the administration office. He wouldn't be back for the rest of the day and so she had gone to the niche in the wall and removed the cell phone. It was now switched on and on silent mode, tucked down the front of her jeans and held in place by the waistband of her panties. During the numerous 'inspection visits' by the Al Khaansa they had never been subjected to a body search and she was aware that this was not the time not to take risks.

Zahi kept taking the cell phone out and checking the screen, holding her breath every time she did so, and this time there was a text from her brother:

> *'He should be there anytime now onwards, go to the gates and watch out for a white-and-tan truck. I am sending his picture for identification. Do exactly as he says.'*

This was it, Zahi thought, and suddenly it was difficult to breathe and her heart thudded heavily inside her chest. She walked to the door and put on her sneakers, her fingers clumsy in her haste, finally managing to tie the laces. It seemed to take an eternity. She didn't look around the house and took nothing with her but the cell phone clutched in her hand, the picture of a young and good-looking man on the screen. Zahi walked to the gate of the house and stood looking out through the bars.

Five minutes passed, and nothing. She stood staring at the empty stretch of road in front of her. A motorcycle and two cars had gone by, and some pedestrians, and yet no truck. Zahi looked at the cell phone again, looked at the picture and then the time. Ten minutes now. Then she saw it. The cabin was white and there was a broad tan stripe running down the body. The truck stopped directly opposite the gate and the man in the picture looked out at her. She opened the gate, flinching at the grating sound it always made, and walked towards the now open cabin door. A large hand reached down, and she grasped it, and a second later she was in the truck. The good-looking driver held out a phone to her and she saw her brother's picture on the screen. He was standing in front of their house. Zahi nodded at the driver and he jerked his head towards the rear. There were three men sitting on a bunk behind the driver and they quickly stood up as the girl entered the cabin. One of the men lifted the seat panel of the bunk and revealed a storage compartment two feet deep and about seven feet long. The girl understood immediately and stepped in. A moment later the panel closed above Zahi and the men took their places on it. The truck moved forward.

Inside the storage space, Zahi found it surprisingly comfortable. It was a large-enough space for her, and there was light filtering in through a line of holes that were drilled a couple of inches down the exterior panel. It was easy to breathe and besides, she had the cell phone for illumination if required. The men in the cabin didn't talk amongst each other and she wondered where they were going. Forty minutes later, the truck stopped and she heard voices from outside it. Although she couldn't hear what was being said, she recognized the rough arrogant tones of the security police, and she held her breath during the verbal exchange that followed. A deep calm voice, which she instinctively guessed was that of the driver, answered the questions at the checkpoint. *Yes, they had passes, here they were*. The rustle of paper followed. *Yes, it was 15 tons of industrial scrap, these men were loaders, yes they have papers too, would you like to see them*, more rustle of paper, *yes, yes thank you brother, Allah be with you. Salaam*, and with a grinding of gears they were off again. Zahi started to shake uncontrollably.

An hour later, the truck slowed and the engine grew louder, as if they had entered a building, and then it was very quiet, with the engine turned off. There was a scraping sound and the top of the storage space was lifted and hands reached in to help her out of the truck and she stood up on unsteady legs. Someone handed her a bottle of water and she gulped it down greedily, as if she had been thirsty for days.

A thickset, bearded man of about forty-five approached her, a broad white-toothed smile on his face. Zahi looked around and saw that she was in a warehouse-like structure with stacks of crates everywhere. The man spoke: 'My name is Dilawar

Choudhary. Here is someone who wants to talk to you,' and he handed her the phone

'Hello.'

'Zahi?' the voice was low, almost conversational, and somehow familiar to her. 'I am your brother's friend and I want you to listen to me carefully, do you understand?'

'Yes,' she replied, 'yes, I understand.'

'The man who handed you this phone is going to get you out of Syria. He and his friends are risking their lives for this, and I want you to obey his every instruction promptly, and trust them implicitly. Only then do we have a chance of pulling this off, is that clear?'

'Yes,' Zahi answered and began to say, 'When will I—'

'Dilawar will explain everything to you,' the Contact broke in. 'I will meet you later. There is very little time, so remember what I say and everything will be fine. I will pass a message to your brother. When it is safer, you can call him yourself. Now give the phones to Dilawar, this one, and the other that you carry.'

Dilawar took the phone from her and moved away. Zahi watched as he spoke in low undertones. Then the stocky man hung up and walked up to a tool rack. Picking up a hammer he proceeded to crush Zahi's phone, the one that had served as a lifeline between her and her brother. She numbly watched him sweep up the pieces and throw them into a garbage bin. The tall handsome man came up to her and spoke in surprisingly fluent English, 'My name is Yasser, please come with me.'

Zahi followed the man through a doorway and into another section of the building. There was a blue van parked there and she followed him to the door. Yasser gestured for her to get in and she entered the van, stopping abruptly at the sight of the occupants.

Raqqa

It was time for Aabir to leave and he had already met his brother Munsiu and his sisters. He would get in touch with them later, but it wouldn't be for several weeks, perhaps even a month or two. They understood that and he saw the pride in their eyes. Aabir made his way to the house, he had to collect his stuff, and then Abu Moumin would send someone to accompany him to the oil trucks. The first part of his journey would be with the convoy of oil trucks to Turkey.

Aabir stepped through the gates and entered the house; he went up to his room and took the suitcase from the wardrobe. He removed the key from his wallet, unlocked the interlinked bottom slides and unzipped it. He examined the contents and nodded in satisfaction. He reached into his robe and withdrew a thick wad of currency which he placed between the shirts and then locked the suitcase again.

The young man looked around his room and then slowly walked down to the living room, carrying the suitcase. Zahi was nowhere to be seen, he hoped that she would return before he had to leave. Abu Moumin's guy would be here shortly. Something occurred to him and he picked up his phone, walked into Munsiu's room and placed it on his brother's desk. He would have to ditch the phone anyway, as he had been instructed, so it was better that his brother had an extra. He was about to turn away when he saw the black handbag. It was Zahi's. He frowned. His sister-in-law never left the house without it. Aabir shrugged. She must have taken one of her other bags. Women and their endless fascination for handbags! he smiled, and went back to the living room. Once more, he looked around the house. He knew he wouldn't be back here and he felt strangely sad. There was a honking at the gates, and he hurried out, closing the door behind him. Aabir swiftly walked up to the car and got in, looking down the street in the hope of spotting Zahi. He would have liked to meet her before leaving.

Baniyas, Syria

The *Star of the East* was about 70 nautical miles off the Syrian coastline, and Captain Brar was happy with the way things had gone so far. His chief officer and the second mate had been briefed, both men had sailed with him for years and he knew he could depend upon them. The second mate had conducted the drill rehearsals twice, and the team had performed satisfactorily, if a bit puzzled. They had, no doubt, put it down to the captain's occasional eccentricities and complied with good humour.

The captain checked the charts again, and the coordinates for the tenth time. He glanced at the clock and made a notation. He nodded, there was nothing else he could do now. A while later, he handed charge of the bridge over to his capable chief and went belowdecks to his cabin. All he could do now was wait—and that was something he was not good at.

Raqqa

Munsiu was having a hurried lunch. It had been a very busy morning so far, and it didn't look like the rest of the day was going to be any different. He had hardly left his desk once, and his back had begun to ache from sitting in that uncomfortable chair. Abbu had left an hour ago and they hadn't had got any time to talk, actually, no time to think. Munsiu finished the last of his rice and walked across to the row of sinks to wash his hands. He returned to his work station and saw that the pile of papers had appreciably increased during his 15-minute absence. With a sigh he sat down at the desk and picked up his phone. He scrolled for his wife's number, dialled and listened to the ringing. After several rings it was apparent that she wasn't going to answer. She'd probably left the phone upstairs and was in the kitchen. Typical of her, he thought, with mild irritation. She would call back once she saw his missed call. He placed the phone aside. Munsiu picked up the next invoice printout and tapped the laptop out of sleep mode. Soon he was totally immersed in his work, the phone lying on the desk, forgotten.

United States

The Contact was back in his house. He reckoned he was safe there for a few days. Eventually, he would have to move. That was inevitable, given that the Islamic State now knew his identity and obviously his address, but not yet. It wasn't that urgent, he thought. Mark tended to agree that he wasn't *that* important and besides, he seriously doubted their ability to have another go at him so soon. So he had decided against an agency safe house, and Mark had to be content with an arrangement with Lieutenant Eggleston to increase patrolling in the vicinity until more permanent arrangements were made. He however insisted that the Contact apply for a concealed carry permit, and that was being rushed through.

The Contact had just got off the phone with Idris, and he looked at the digital clock. It had been three hours since the pickup and there were a few hours yet to pass. He picked up a book. It was a biography of Albert Einstein, and he began to read it. From time to time, he glanced at the clock.

Maldives

Ahmed Idris stood on the balcony and looked out at the night. He was trying not to fidget too much and had avoided walking around the house. That would disturb is wife and the kids. His wife wanted to know why he was upset, so he had told her that he needed to be up to take some international calls. The Contact had briefed him and he knew that Zahi was on the road now, that was all he knew and so he stood on the balcony trying to keep his mind from inventing worst- and best-case scenarios and prayed that the time would pass quicker.

Syria

The van had already been stopped twice and each time they had got away, the papers were holding up and the searches had concentrated on contraband rather than people. On that front, the image they presented was authentic. Dilawar the spice trader sat in front next to the driver and he did all the talking. The last checkpoint had a unit of Al Khaansa but they had addressed Yasser's wife and she had replied to their queries, *Yes they were a family and there was a marriage to be arranged, hence the suitcases of fine clothes and gifts and thank you for your good wishes, Allah be praised.*

Zahi sat in the middle seat with Dilawar's wife at her side and the toddler on her lap. The van had been allowed to pass, the tension in the vehicle had palpably decreased and the toddler chattered on, oblivious to the silent drama around him. Yasser followed a mile behind them, with three of their best men. Dilawer's thumb came off his mobile. If they were to be stopped and detained, Yasser was to come up and they would take it from there. Most checkpoints were manned by 6 to 8 soldiers, and given the element of surprise, and some luck, they could make a break for it. It was chancy, they knew, and there were bound to be casualties. The spice trader hoped fervently that it wouldn't come to that. But so far, their luck had held, and there were those machine pistols taped under the dashboards, and he had the two grenades among the small pile of cleaning rags in the door recess. The driver increased speed and the blue van resumed its journey. Behind them Yasser and his boys negotiated the checkpoint and stayed behind them. Two hours later, they reached Baniyas.

CHAPTER TWENTY

The silver lines advanced steadily, the distance between them widening as they came closer and then they bulged outwards till they formed a semicircle before bursting into a thousand pyramid-shaped splashes and the sound came two seconds later, a deep boom, as the waves broke and then, long seconds of near silence while the shoreline receded with a barely audible hiss over the sands.

They stood thirty metres above the small inlet barely a hundred yards wide. It was a place the spice trader had used before, a lonely desolate strip of sand, where a fast motorboat could come within 25 metres off the shore line and not run aground. Zahi shivered slightly as a gust of cold air momentarily buffeted them. The women and the toddler had gone hours ago and she once more felt humbled by the kindness of strangers. May Allah bless them and watch over them, she prayed again, may the little one live a hundred years. They had left accompanied by two of Yasser's men and Zahi had watched the blue van go away and wondered how she would even begin to repay the debt if she ever got out of this alive.

She looked sideways and up at the men who flanked her, the stocky spice trader and his handsome son Yasser. She wasn't introduced to the other men and they were spread out over a distance, no doubt following a drill that indicated a long familiarity with guns and danger. Another boom reverberated upwards and this time she saw a yellow flash down below and out there, and Dilawar turned to his son.

'That's Kemal. You leave now and I will meet up with you at home.' Yasser clasped his father by the arms tightly and then melted away into the darkness followed by his men, and Zahi followed the spice trader down the slight gradient that led down to the tiny bay. She had discarded the hijab and wore jeans and a thick jacket over a sweatshirt. Going down was easy, although the stocky Dilawar had to hold her arm a couple of times to steady her. Above them, Yasser had already started walking towards the truck, when something made him stop and turn around.

Zahi's sneakers touched sand and the speedboat was plainly visible now. They started to hurry towards it and that's when their luck ran out...

The Syrian border patrol had stumbled on the place by pure chance. It was a three-man unit on a routine shoreline patrol. They were bored and they had seen the light flashing close to the shore 200 yards away, so they had stopped to observe. Maybe the corporal reckoned... this could prove to be profitable. They watched as the two figures half-walked, half-ran through the shadows and over the sand and into the water and leaned forward, slowing as the sea pushed them back and then, the unit saw the line of the hips and realized that the shorter one was a woman. The corporal spoke softly to his men, ordering them to fire a warning shot and thereafter aim for the legs, while he raised his own rifle to his shoulder and aimed for the speedboat. A second later, the night was punctuated by gunfire and the two figures desperately lunged towards the boat, the spice trader reaching it first, and Kemal hoisting him aboard. Dilawar Choudhary bent forward and reached out to help the girl, when the firing intensified, and then his legs lost strength because he was hit. The girl cried out and their hands slithered off each other, and now the boat was moving away, with the girl shrinking in the distance, and everything seemed to move so slowly. The spice trader sank down to the deck, thinking *we were so close, so close*—and then his head exploded in pain and everything went black.

Unites States

Mark Ross was at the Contact's house but the man wasn't home. The neighbour informed him that the the dog was in a kennel and they fed the fish twice a day. The FBI agent looked around at the motley collection of furniture that the Contact had chosen for his house and shook his head. The obviously valuable antique rolltop desk was totally at odds with the five-dollar sad excuse for a chair. It had either come with the house or bought at a Sunday parking lot flea market. The agent had tried calling the number but it had been switched off. That was the day before, so Mark had driven over to give him the news about the Raqqa thing. A call to the kennel revealed that the dog had been checked in for a week's stay and currently in good health. The package at the dog's inn included two exercise periods of half an hour each every day, which the animal had seemed to enjoy. The Contact had left the neighbour's number as the emergency contact detail. Oh, well, thought the agent, I will probably see him next week and will tell him then. He left his card and a message on the rolltop.

The Star of the East

The second mate was a man who minded his own business, but the entire episode would make any man curious. He had taken the watch an hour ago, and his thoughts repeatedly went back to the curious incident. It had been a few days since the night they had taken on the passenger. The rescue crew had responded to an emergency drill yet again, only, this time, it was for real, and the boat had pulled up alongside a small speed-boat in the water that had switched off all its lights. It had been dark on deck, too, as per the captain's orders, and so they hadn't been able to see much of the passenger pulled aboard, but it had definitely been a girl. The chief had personally assisted her in helping her out of the harness and then she had been hustled below deck. Nobody had seen her since and the captain's quarters had been off limits this last week.

As for the speedboat, it hadn't hung around. Indeed, the two men had sped off as soon as the girl had been taken aboard. The second mate wasn't sure, but he could have sworn that one of the men moved as if he was injured in some manner. The whole thing was very curious, yes, but then he wasn't one to poke his nose into matters that didn't concern him. He liked it on board the *Star of the East*, the boss was fair, the pay was great, and that, thought the second mate, was that.

Mumbai, India

The immigration officer was waiting for his relief and sighed as he saw the fresh deluge of passengers that had just landed. The queues formed swiftly and the young lady with the pert nose and expensive haircut placed her passport on the counter. The immigration officer examined the document, noting the departure date, and then looked at the photograph and then again at the passenger. This one had obviously spent some time on the beach, going by the tan. She smiled at him and he noticed again how pretty she was. He smiled back and handed the passport back to her. The next one in line was a tall man in a corduroy jacket. The immigration officer gestured to him and the man stepped to the counter.

Raqqa

Abu Moumin al Fransisi walked through the still-smoking ruins of what used to be the house. The gate was just a twisted pretzel of cast iron that hung brokenly from a column of brick and mortar. The main structure of the house itself was totally demolished and even the compound wall was mostly gone, a small shed in a corner somehow remained miraculously intact. There had been no survivors, Abu Moumin had been informed, indeed the only things found had been a few charred bits of remains which were totally unidentifiable. The houses on both sides had escaped unscathed, except for broken glass and discoloured walls. The hit had been delivered with pinpoint accuracy as if it had been guided by exact coordinates or… Abu Moumin thought, they had been homing in on a signal.

And yet they had missed, he thought, and they didn't know it. He looked up at the sky and saw nothing except a cerulean stretch of blue. The soldier shrugged and started picking his way back to the waiting jeep. There was much to be done and besides, there was nothing here for him now.

Epilogue

Mark Ross came out of the holding cell and walked to his desk. He had just finished questioning a suspect in a money-laundering case and wanted to draft the statement. He settled into his chair, checked his office inbox out of pure habit, and noticed an update from the interception unit. One of the numbers they had been tracking from the Raqqa thing had been inactive for two weeks now and they were taking it off the watchlist. Mark thought back on the case. They had gleaned a lot of valuable intel during the period and some of it was still being monitored. He was not directly involved anymore, it was in the hands of the analysts. Now, he was a more detection and hands-on type of guy, and longtime monitoring and analysis weren't his forte.

The agent's thoughts turned towards the Contact. The last time they had met was all those months ago when he had visited the man to tell him about the family. The Contact had listened to him and, all the while keeping a noncommittal expression on his face. 'Well, I suppose it couldn't be helped,' was all he had said, and then politely thanked Mark for his help and update.

Mark Ross had then come to the point that bothered him and his section chief. 'You never really told me where you had gone for a week. It was right around the time everything came to a head.'

The Contact had reached into his trouser pocket and taken out a memory stick and handed it over to the agent, who looked at him questioningly.

'One of the family was working in the Islamic State headquarters. This is a list of bank accounts, shell companies and details of cash transfer routes. The girl managed to pass it on to her brother.' The Contact looked Mark in the eye and simply said, 'I was in Dubai, shopping for some shirts, so let's leave it at that shall we?'

Mark had understood that the man was telling him not to look the gift horse in the mouth, and not to ask questions if he was not going to like the answers. Mark had nodded and pocketed the memory stick, and the two men had parted with the agent driving away and the rearview mirror reflecting a tall, wide-shouldered man watching him leave.

The contents of the memory stick had sent the section chief into raptures. Yet, Mark wondered sometimes, where had the man truly been? And what had he actually done there? Mark had considered calling a couple of times in the last few months, but for some reason he had hesitated. Wouldn't hurt to say 'Hi,' he thought, maybe have a drink together one of these days. But for now the agent had his statement to draft and so he pulled the keyboard nearer and started typing.

***

Sameer Ibraheem divides his time equally between Malé and Kalinidhoo. His mother's health is failing and he worries about that. He knows what happened in Raqqa, word reached him through some of Munsiu's friends, and for the next few months he had been beside himself with grief. He still has difficulty processing the why and how of his siblings' actions and sometimes he has to take long walks around the island. His wife watches him and her heart breaks at her man's grief. His son is growing and he is the only one who makes Sameer smile. He meets Ahmed Idris sometimes, but their conversation is strained and they tend to say premature goodbyes.

But things are getting better and the police don't bother him with visits anymore. He has opened a shop of novelty items in the capital, and his wife runs it happily. Next week they were going for a vacation to Singapore and his wife was looking forward to that. For Sameer, life wasn't perfect, but it was slowly getting better.

***

Dilawar Choudhary had healed within a fortnight. The bullet had grazed his temple and the concussion had made him unsteady for a couple of days, but that was months ago, and the spice trader was fully recovered now. The memory of the wild breakneck run in the coal-black night with the speedboat bucking under their feet still thrills him. The Contact had visited last month and had stayed the weekend. It had been a good visit and the household had been sorry to see him go. The spice trader was in his house in Oman and insisted that he had officially retired. His son Yasser would look after the business now and he, Dilawar, would now be content at home and could now stop to smell the roses.

His wife doesn't believe him.

***

Mohsin Shameem, the Escort, died on the sands of Syria. He died with blood in his mouth, and his body was given a hasty and shallow burial by the others. They had been escorting a new batch of recruits when the Syrian air force jets had dived out of the sun and raked the small convoy. As the others salvaged what they could out of the wreckage, they found the Escort's binoculars, a fine bit of merchandise and fit for a desert warrior. His friends gave them to Mohsin's younger brother. He carries them now, and they come in handy.

***

Captain Lakhwinder (Jolly) Brar is still the master of the *Star of the East* and he still does the occasional oil run, why not? He thinks the money is good and the risk is acceptable. He plans to retire but not for a few years yet. He reckons he will settle in Canada, he has a daughter there and for some time now she has been urging him to shift over there. The idea is growing on him.

***

Abu Nasser, the Moviemaker, keeps making his movies but of late, the funds are slow to come in. He makes do with the resources available to him and enjoys the appreciation of the Islamic State. He has just put the finishing touches to a bunch of slides that will be used as a study app in schools, and his next project is a series of GIFs that could help spread the message of the soon-to-be caliphate. The Moviemaker is content with his duties. He has no desire to venture into the outside world. He has experienced it, and found it wanting. For him life is best viewed through the lens of a camera.

***

Ahmed Idris's business is flourishing, and he has opened up offices in two other countries. There is a spring in his step, but his eyes have a habit of staring into nothing at times, and he thinks his wife doesn't notice. At first, she misunderstood when she noticed that he seemed happier after he returned from his regular business trips abroad; she suspected that he had a mistress somewhere. Then, one evening, he sat her down and talked for a long time, and it was as if a weight has lifted off him. Idris knows he is a very lucky man, he has the wealth of gold and the treasure of friends and family, and he will never take any of them for granted again.

***

Zahi has another name now and sometimes she forgets to look up when someone calls out to her, but it happens less frequently these days. She is amongst friends and good people and the city is vibrant. She has a job in an advertising firm and shares a flat with two other girls. Sometimes, her friends find her distant and disconnected, but they are used to that; they sense a past and are too decent to probe. She is grateful for that.

She thinks of Munsiu sometimes, and the others, and most days it all seems to be in the distant past, but on some days she is back in Raqqa again, and the walls start closing in on her, and on days like that she needs her brother. Her mother had visited and it was wonderful, but it couldn't happen very often. It was too dangerous, and that was how it was always going to be; that was the truth that was so hard to bear.

***

Shaikh Adnan Shakeel continues to run the Salaf and propagate the Islamic State's agenda in the Maldives. He skilfully weaves the thread of Salafist ideology into the fabric of Maldivian society and politics. Every few weeks, another misguided soul is given an address, a telephone number, a thin wad of currency, and handed a ticket to Syria.

***

Aabir keeps to himself. He is pleasant enough when someone engages him in conversation, and the girls generally try to make eye contact with him. He lives in a small apartment in the better section of the city and attends classes regularly; his professors are impressed with his keen mind and natural aptitude for all things mechanical, especially aeronautical. Every month an allowance gets deposited in his bank account and he spends it carefully. The young man works out daily in the neighbourhood fitness centre. He doesn't drink or smoke, and he reads the Holy Book and prays with all his heart. He is waiting.

***

The Contact has moved to a new house. It's a modest cottage in a nice quiet neighbourhood with tall leafy oaks, and there are walking trails nearby. The people in the locality have grown accustomed to the sight of the tall, quiet man with the large dog. The Contact knows that his identity is known to the Islamic State and he has taken precautions. He is not unduly worried, but he isn't complacent either. Some evenings, the Contact thinks about Ahmed Idris and his sister, and he is glad he could help his friend.

He has a bigger pond now, and this time he has opted for a custom-built filter. It works just fine. The koi still don't eat out of his hand but one day, he hopes, they will.